SPECIAL CHILDREN

MEETING THE CHALLENGE IN THE PRIMARY SCHOOL

Jane Leadbetter and Peter Leadbetter

CASSELL

Cassell
Villiers House   387 Park Avenue South
41/47 Strand   New York, NY 10016-8810
London WC2N 5JE   USA

British Library Cataloguing-in-Publication Data
A catalogue record for this book is available from the British Library.

Library of Congress Cataloging-in-Publication Data
Leadbetter, Jane, 1954–
    Special children: meeting the challenge in the primary school/
Jane Leadbetter and Peter Leadbetter.
        p.   cm. – (Introduction to education)
    Includes bibliographical references and index.
    ISBN 0-304-32522-8 – 0-304-32524-4 (pbk.)
        1. Handicapped children – Education (Primary) – Great Britain.
    2. Special education – Great Britain.   I. Leadbetter, Peter, 1952–
II. Title.   III. Series.
    LC4031.L395   1993
    371.9'0973 – dc20   92-38452
                                                        CIP

ISBN 0-304-32522-8 (hardback)
        0-304-32524-4 (paperback)

Typeset by Colset Private Limited, Singapore
Printed and bound in Great Britain
by Biddles Ltd, Guildford and King's Lynn

To our children, Chloe and Rory, and to the memory of their grandfather, Dr Reg Cotterhill, who inspired us both.

CONTENTS

FOREWORD

The 1980s and 1990s have witnessed unprecedented changes to the education system. These have had a dramatic impact, particularly in relation to:

- schools' relationships with parents and the community;
- the funding and management of schools;
- the curriculum;
- the assessment of children's learning.

It can be an extremely daunting task for student teachers to unravel the details and implications of these initiatives. This Introduction to Education series therefore offers a comprehensive analysis and evaluation of educational theory and practice in the light of recent developments.

The series examines topics and issues of concern to those entering the teaching profession. Major themes representing a spectrum of educational opinion are presented in a clear, balanced and analytic manner.

The authors in the series are authorities in their field. They emphasize the need to have a well-informed and critical teaching profession and present a positive and optimistic view of the teacher's role. They endorse the view that teachers have a significant influence over the extent to which any legislation or ideology is translated into effective classroom practice.

Each author addresses similar issues, which can be summarized as:

- presenting and debating theoretical perspectives within appropriate social, political, and educational contexts;
- identifying key arguments;

- identifying individuals who have made significant contributions to the field under review;
- discussing and evaluating key legislation;
- critically evaluating research and highlighting implications for classroom practice;
- providing an overview of the current state of debate within each field;
- describing the features of good practice.

The books are written primarily for student teachers. However, they will be of interest and value to all those involved in education.

Jonathan Solity
Series Editor

ACKNOWLEDGEMENTS

We are indebted to our friend and editor, Jonathan Solity, who persuaded us that this was a project we could achieve and supported us throughout the endeavour. His critical feedback and guidance often helped us when there appeared to be more wood than trees. We always felt encouraged by his sureness and sense of purpose, particularly when the demands were hard from children and the book at the same time.

We are also grateful to our psychologist and teacher colleagues in Birmingham, whose stimulating comments have helped shape the ideas and views which are the substance of this book. The teachers and children with whom we have worked have offered the encouragement to pursue initiatives and the feedback against which we have measured the feasibility of our views. We alone, however, accept responsibility for any errors which may appear in this book.

CHAPTER 1

Introduction

OUR APPROACH

Primary schools in the United Kingdom are made up of children of all shapes, sizes, talents and abilities. They come from a range of ethnic, cultural, linguistic and economic backgrounds to attend schools which now follow a commonly agreed curriculum and within which they will be assessed against nationally agreed criteria. In every class there will be some children whose individual differences or circumstances mean that they have special educational needs, as defined in the broadest of terms. The combination of children with a huge range of abilities and prescribed programmes of study could cause grave problems for children and teachers alike, and it is the challenging process of assimilating the needs of children with school and curriculum requirements that provides the focus of this book.

Our approach to the teaching of children with special needs is essentially positive. We do not view special needs teaching as any different from any other good teaching practice. If a teacher, in whatever context, can accurately assess a child's present skills, provide appropriate programmes of work, is sensitive to factors in the teaching environment which might affect the child, and is able to provide sufficient motivation, then this represents good teaching, regardless of whether or not it is considered 'special'.

OUR AIMS

We see this book as a mixture of introductory primer, handbook and reference source for primary school teachers. In it we have aimed to give a general introduction to pertinent issues in the education of children with special educational needs; a more detailed look at the groups of such children most often encountered by primary teachers (i.e. those with learning difficulties and those with behaviour problems); and some background information on relevant topics, including the needs of particular groups of children, the situation of pre-school children and the effects of legislation and policy-making on special-needs teaching. Our underlying concern has been *to illuminate important issues, give practical ideas for use in the classroom* and *provide useful information on related topics.*

PHILOSOPHICAL PERSPECTIVE

Many books have been written about the changing concepts of special educational needs, and most of them include a historical survey of special education and special needs teaching. Undoubtedly, views have changed significantly on the nature of children's disabilities and how these affect their education. However, we have not chosen to dwell on the historical perspective, preferring instead to compare special needs teaching with the models that inform contemporary mainstream teaching. This is in line with the move away from focusing on children's disabilities towards identifying their special educational needs: a positive shift in viewpoint that allows children to be seen as individuals with particular strengths and weaknesses and, in some cases, particular conditions and disabilities which lead to their having special requirements. It also shows that teachers do not need to reconstruct their teaching approach purely because they have individuals in their class with difficulties. Instead, they can aim to modify their existing practice in certain aspects, perhaps in terms of lesson planning or classroom organization, in order to meet the needs of particular children.

This perspective allows us to hope that, despite the massive and continual changes in education, our discussion and the advice we offer will always be found relevant.

AN OUTLINE OF CHAPTER CONTENT

Chapter 2 sets the scene for the rest of the book, by considering the thorny issue of integration and the ideas that inform the arguments for and against. The integration of children with special needs into mainstream schools is compared with the experiences of other groups who have been brought into mainstream or community settings. Since integration can mean different things, consideration is given to the range of possible provision. Finally, the benefits of successful programmes of integration are considered, as are the possible drawbacks.

Chapters 3 and 4 are both concerned with the large group of children who have some degree of learning difficulty. In Chapter 3 we look at definitions of the term 'learning difficulty' and, in particular, highlight the dangers of comparing too closely the achievements of one child with another. Chapter 4 has a more practical orientation and contains advice and ideas for classroom use. The model of assessment-through-teaching is described and recommended as a useful approach, particularly for children with learning difficulties.

Chapters 5 and 6 also form a pair, and are concerned with another large group of children, many of whom spend their whole school careers in mainstream classrooms: those with emotional and/or behavioural difficulties. Chapter 5 looks at what it is that makes certain children's behaviour problematic for teachers. The findings of the Elton Report (1989) are considered and some of the approaches employed to help such children are surveyed. A behavioural approach is described, and proposed as a good starting-point for effective classroom management. Chapter 6 presents a problem-solving model and demonstrates how teachers using this can systematically influence the behaviour of others. Practical guidance on the use of rules, rewards, sanctions and specific classroom techniques is included here.

Chapter 7 is about other groups of children with special needs: those with hearing or visual impairment, physical difficulties, severe learning difficulties, autistic features and, finally, language and communication problems. For each of these groups some general information about the disability or condition is given, along with a critical analysis of the broad educational issues and some indication of the implications for teachers.

Chapter 8 provides some insight for the primary teacher into the lives of pre-school children who are experiencing difficulties. With its emphasis on looking at the situation from the viewpoint of the child and the parents, it has relevance for the education of similar children of school age. The importance of positive intervention in the lives of children is emphasized and the model of parental support offered by the Portage scheme is recommended.

In Chapter 9 we evaluate the effects of policy making on the lives of children with special needs with reference to important recent legislation: the Education Act 1981, the Education Reform Act 1988 and the Children Act 1989. Political shifts and new legislation have altered the role of local education authorities; we try to indicate the significance of these changes for special needs provision, finally moving on to policy-making at local school and individual teacher level. A model of policy development is described which may be of use in clarifying the rationale and practice of special needs policy in schools.

Our final chapter attempts to speculate on what the future may hold for children with special needs. More specifically, it considers what secondary schooling holds for these children, both in terms of strengths and weaknesses. The process of transfer is crucial, and so we look at what primary schools can do to make it as easy as possible.

We hope that teachers will find much in this book which is useful to them, whether it is a snippet of information that saves them a trip to the nearest reference library or a practical solution to a troublesome classroom situation. We would like to think that if it helps the teacher, it is likely to help, too, a particular child with special needs.

The field of special education is a fascinating and challenging one. We commend it to all teachers.

CHAPTER 2

Integration: principles, problems and practice

CHAPTER OVERVIEW

This chapter examines the issue of integration and shows the divergence between what may seem a straightforward concept and the complex and emotive reality. We analyse the arguments for and against integration, and indicate the various forms that positive integration can take. Finally, we look at the challenges that integration presents for teachers, before speculating over possible future trends.

Our viewpoint is as close as possible to that of the child and the teacher. All too often, writers seem to focus on beliefs, ideologies and politics, so that the real needs and the views of children and their families become almost incidental. We link the discussion to developments in other aspects of work with people with special needs and related issues from recent history.

SETTING THE SCENE

Commenting on the likely impact of the 1981 Education Act, shortly after its publication, senior educationalists and commentators predicted that the ensuing ten years would see a major swing towards the integration of children with special needs into mainstream schools and the likely demise of all but a few special schools. These strong predictions have not been fulfilled and, although the number and proportion of pupils going into segregated special education have fallen slightly since 1981, the goal of significant levels of integration seems as unattainable as it ever was (Table 2.1). The *Times Educational*

Table 2.1 The number (000s) and percentage of pupils being educated in special schools

School year	Number of pupils in all UK schools	Number of pupils in special schools	Percentage of pupils in special education
1980/81	10,525.3	147.2	1.40%
1985/86	9,384.8	130.0	1.39%
1988/89	9,022.7	117.6	1.30%
1989/90	9,010.0	114.6	1.27%

Source: Department of Education and Science (1991)

Supplement (1 May 1992) quoted a research report from the Centre for Studies of Integration in Education:

> the pace of integration is too slow. Only 100 Special schools have been closed; 100,000 children are still segregated. (p. 12)

Integration in the social context

In general, there is increasing social awareness of how we have excluded, and often still do exclude, people with special needs from social activities. When a new building is designed, due emphasis now has to be given to ensuring access for people with physical disabilities. Entertainment centres, such as cinemas and theatres, are increasingly fitting loops so that customers with hearing difficulties can use their radio aids successfully. Playgrounds are built to ensure that wheelchair-bound children can participate. There thus seems to be some recognition of how, in physical terms alone, we have been discriminating against, or at least not discriminating in favour of, people with special needs. Discrimination against people on the grounds of race, gender or sexuality is not only becoming socially unacceptable, it is prohibited by law.

In view of all this, surely pupils with special needs should be finding readier access to non-segregated education? Yet this is far from the case, despite the 1981 Education Act, which was regarded as the piece of legislation that would enable the recommendations and aspirations of the Warnock Report to take tangible form. Goacher *et al.* (1988, p. 151), surveying the impact of the Act, wrote:

> The right of children with special educational needs to receive their education in ordinary schools, mixing with children who do not have special educational needs, is the way in which the 1981 Education Act codifies the principles of equality of opportunity and the right to education in the least restrictive environment . . .

A challenge had definitely been made to the established practice of educating children, who in some way were *different*, in *different* schools.

In this the Act was in line with legislation aimed at reducing the segregation of other social groups. The era of long-stay hospitals for the mentally ill and handicapped is passing as such people are placed back into the community, where they can be supported on a community care basis. The legislation for achieving this, particularly the Community Care Act 1990, owed much to the idea that such patients had specific *rights* which entitled them to as normal a life-style as possible, and one which was not isolated from the remainder of the community. The case for integration of special needs groups within education has a similar philosophical basis.

Again the underlying concern has to do with individual rights: on what premise can a child be denied the opportunity of doing what other children take for granted, which, in the case of special needs children, means attending a local mainstream school? This makes the issue sound straightforward. It is not so, because children's *rights* are not the only considerations; their *needs* must also be taken into account. We will return to these issues in more detail later in the chapter (pp. 11–13).

There are common themes between the integration of special needs pupils and the integration of racial minorities into mainstream schools in the United States, an issue that formed part of the civil rights struggle. Educational apartheid is no longer accepted in the United States, the principle of equal rights having been enshrined in legislation. The 'bussing' issue created great social unrest during the Kennedy presidency as black children from socially disadvantaged homes were transported to schools in the more affluent white areas of major cities and towns. The rationale was that the black children had a right to be compensated for their social disadvantage through attending better resourced schools, where standards were generally much higher and from which, it was argued, they would benefit academically, linguistically and socially. Black children, it was argued, had been prevented from participating in the most socially and academically beneficial schools; they had been discriminated against and made to feel inferior by their segregation.

It can be argued that segregation has also discriminated against special needs pupils in the UK. Many are disadvantaged by their disabilities or learning problems and, despite the best efforts of special schools to offer high-quality education, they cannot, it is argued, supply children with an important source of learning, namely that provided by contact with mainstream children. From this position the argument progressed to insisting that all children have a right on moral and educational grounds to attend a mainstream school unless all relevant parties agree that it would be in the individual's best interests to be educated in a special school or unit. Informed choice for parents is a key element in the case for allowing special needs children into mainstream education.

The current situation

What is the current situation in schools in the UK? Following their survey into the impact of the 1981 Education Act, Goacher *et al.* (1988, p. 149) concluded that LEAs had become more aware of the existence of special needs pupils and accepted their obligation to meet these needs:

> This awareness . . . manifested itself in a substantial increase in the proportion of children with special educational needs receiving education in mainstream schools . . .

'Substantial' is, of course, a relative term. In the context of expectations raised by the 1981 Act it means little, and full integration of all pupils into mainstream schools is still a long way off. In reviewing the research recently published by the Centre for Studies on Integration in Education, Hall (1992, p. 20) concluded:

> the overwhelming majority of LEAs have made very poor progress towards the goal of full inclusion and some are actually increasing the proportion of their pupils in segregated settings.

Why the current situation has developed will be discussed below (pp. 17–20). In general, we share the perspective taken by Hegarty (1987), who feels that the cause of integration would be furthered by changing the focus of debate from the need for a child to be integrated to the need for the school to change to accommodate him.* We also agree with Hegarty when he suggests that schools which fail their special needs pupils are likely also to be failing many others.

EXAMINING THE CONCEPT OF INTEGRATION

Integration is a concept rather than something that can be achieved by following a clearly prescribed set of practical guidelines in cookbook fashion. Integration is not an all-or-nothing state of affairs, in the sense that a particular school or LEA can meaningfully be described as 'integrationist', nor does it mean much to say that a child is 'integrated' into a particular school or situation. Integration is a value-laden concept in that it reflects the value systems of individual teachers

---

*For convenience, the pronoun 'he' is used throughout to refer in a general sense to a child of either sex. Similarly, teachers, psychologists and others are referred to as 'she'.

and whole schools. There is not necessarily any common understanding of what is involved when the word is used to describe a special needs child's involvement with a mainstream school. What can be done is to examine the situation for a particular child to determine at what levels he is integrated and in which aspects of his school life.

The opposite concept, segregation, is also misleading if it merely conjures up images of isolation and denial, of children being treated differently, of having different lifestyles, of having a restricted range of choices and ultimately a different experience of the community. Such a stark and over-simplified contrast makes segregation appear to be 'bad' whilst integration appears 'good'. In practice, integration itself has to be viewed as a relative concept manifesting itself in a variety of different formats within schools, for a range of reasons.

Integration has to be a working goal that is regularly reassessed in the light of experience; it must be viewed as a dynamic rather than a static concept. At an LEA level, Topping (1983) has argued that this requires a continuum of special provision to match the continuum of special needs. On the basis of Topping's model, a possible range of such provision could include:

- *Mainstream classroom* with pupil treated no differently from peers.
- *Mainstream classroom* with pupil being taught, for all or part of the time, in a small group or on a one to one basis, but always in the classroom and by the class teachers.
- *Mainstream classroom* but with the pupil being supported in the classroom by the school's special needs co-ordinator or by an outside support teacher.
- *Mainstream classroom* with the pupil being withdrawn from the classroom for specialist work by the same support staff.
- *Mainstream classroom* with the pupil spending part of the week in a special school or unit.
- *Unit placement in a mainstream school* with the bulk of the teaching being conducted in the unit, but the child mixing socially and for parts of the curriculum with non-unit pupils.
- *Placement in a special school* on a day basis.
- *Placement in a special school* on a residential basis, either on a termly or on a weekly basis.

This is not a definitive or exhaustive list. It could be made to include team-teaching in a variety of the above situations, and various forms of outreach support from special schools. And any one child might experience a range of the above scenarios during his school career or even one school year.

In reflecting on the various practices, one should bear in mind three dimensions of integration arrangements which were proposed in the

Warnock Report: *locational*, *functional* and *social* integration. A child is *functionally* integrated when he receives a curriculum diet which is broadly similar to that of his peers and is delivered in the classroom. *Locational* integration refers to the possibility of a child being taught on the same site, perhaps in a unit, but being segregated in all other respects. The dimension of *social* integration refers to the degree of social interaction which the child is able to have with his peers during the whole school day. Obviously the degrees of each of these dimensions may vary within and between the arrangements listed above.

The range of provision within an LEA depends on that authority's policies and funding arrangements, though nowadays procedures for meeting the needs of special needs pupils within schools are increasingly being determined by headteachers and governing bodies, albeit in the context of the government's support for integration. Indeed, whether schools decide to admit or to retain particular pupils is no longer wholly determined by the LEA. The Education Act 1986 has given school governors the power to exclude a child if they believe that the school is unable to meet that pupil's needs; and though the LEA still has the power to overrule such decisions, it is a waning power. LEA initiatives are similarly constrained. For example, an LEA seeking to extend its range of special needs provision, by opening a unit for pupils with difficulties within a mainstream school, will now have to persuade the governing body of that school to agree to the plans where previously the LEA would have simply directed the headteacher. Governors are only likely to agree if financial and other incentives, such as agreed levels of support staff input, are adequate.

There are a variety of possible arrangements for special needs children within schools, once there is a real acceptance that securing the maximum levels of integration is in pupils' best interests. Once arrangements for maximizing integration have been set up, it is important to realize the danger of regarding them as static, either within a school or across an LEA. Children should not simply be slotted into the existing arrangements. Ideally, the variability and range of such arrangements should be seen as the means by which a school can 'fine tune' how it meets a child's needs. It is always necessary to consider the pupil as a person with a specific personality and wishes. The Children Act 1989 requires those planning for a 'child in need' to establish the child's wishes and to incorporate these into provision whenever this is possible. It is particularly necessary to bear this requirement in mind when considering the issue of integration. It is all too easy to argue that integration is 'good' for a child and to ignore the pupil's wishes. The arguments surrounding integration need considering in more detail.

THE ARGUMENTS FOR AND AGAINST INTEGRATION

The concept of integration is, as we have seen, a complex one, as too are the arguments underpinning its interpretation. Several commentators have referred to it as a *process*, probably because of the variety of arrangements which are said to represent various forms of integration. In general terms, integration is what goes on when educators seek to provide special needs pupils with a learning environment which most closely matches the child's needs and which is as near to a *normal* school environment as possible. *Normal* is construed to be that which is offered to the vast majority of children, and educators seeking to achieve integration are trying to achieve *normalization* for special needs children. Let us examine the assumptions behind these attempted definitions.

Assumptions behind argument for integration

The first assumption is that anything other than the total integration of all pupils is tantamount to supporting a form of educational apartheid, and is therefore ethically and philosophically unsound. In other words, it is tempting to regard the advantages of integration as on a par with 'apple pie and parenthood', i.e. intrinsically good. This simplistic assumption owes much to the analogy with basic human rights – an analogy that works only up to a certain point. Leaving aside these assumptions, what evidence is there to support the benefit of integration?

The benefits of integration

Societal benefits

If schools' main objective were to secure the highest possible levels of academic achievement, then the arguments about integration would be relatively easily resolved. Thankfully, our schools also seek to fit pupils for life in society and try to provide an education that will enable them to contribute to and live happily within that society. This preparation is especially vital for children with a physical disability, a learning difficulty, behaviour problems or a sensory loss, for they are already, to some extent, isolated from aspects of ordinary life. Their education should not further isolate them. Nor should it devalue the child, as may happen when he is separated from his peers without justifiable cause. This process can label the child as an outsider at a very early stage in his life.

There is another side to this argument, which points to the wider

11

benefits for society of pursuing integration in our schools. All children, it is argued, can achieve a more realistic, sensitive and optimistic view of the capabilities of special needs peers if they are educated and grow up alongside pupils with disabilities. Integration thus ensures a greater degree of understanding, more knowledge about certain disabilities and a generally more positive outlook towards those who have them. The philosophy underpinning such arguments is essentially libertarian tinged with social pragmatism in that it is believed that *all* children would benefit from integration.

Does the evidence support these assertions? It does in schools where there is an active and well-run integration policy. In such settings it is genuinely encouraging to observe physically disabled children, Down's syndrome children and pupils with a myriad of special needs being educated alongside their peers, playing together in the playground and, most importantly, contributing to the overall life of the school. It is also apparent that *all* pupils and of course teachers gain beneficial insights from these ventures. However, it would be naive to suggest that all schools are so successful. Nevertheless, there is a strong argument in favour of pursuing integration if we are seeking to train youngsters in the skills and attitudes which will be necessary to establish a tolerant society which seeks to maximize what all members can contribute, regardless of their disabilities.

The development of overall teaching skills

An adage that will surface at several points in this book, and is particularly relevant at this stage, is that *good special needs teaching or teaching which seeks to meet the demands of a range of special needs pupils is, quite simply, good teaching.* The skills necessary for teaching special needs pupils will have wider pay-offs. The same techniques used to teach a broad curriculum to a child with learning difficulties can be adapted for a pupil who is stuck on a particular concept or skill. If teachers learn to set aside restricted expectations for special needs pupils, those children might achieve more than was initially imagined as possible, and similar gains may perhaps be achieved with a wider range of pupils if the same approaches and techniques are used.

Gains for special needs pupils

The benefits for some special needs pupils of being educated alongside their peers are so evident that one might as well ask, simply, 'What are the benefits of schools?' Natural learning is a part of the wider process of learning which takes place in all schools. Pupils learn from each other, particularly from older children, and they acquire an appreciation of how to behave, in general terms, from more sources than just their teachers. Models of appropriate behaviour can be positive incentives to pupils with behaviour difficulties. Parents of one particular group of special needs pupils, those with Down's syndrome, often refer to the immense benefits gained by their children in learning from and imitating other children in mainstream schools. The language environment, in a mainstream school, will be a rich source of stimulation and modelling for the pupil whose language is delayed; in this context the possibilities for imitational learning are significant.

When reviewing the available research findings in regard to the integration of pupils with severe learning difficulties in mainstream classes, a working party of members of the Association of Educational Psychologists (AEP, 1989, p. 6) reached two interesting conclusions:

> such pupils may show most progress in less 'academic' areas like social skills and communication,

and

> indications are that children learn socially appropriate behaviour through modelling in integrated provision and their play becomes more imaginative. . . . It is also likely that integrated pupils will cope better in society when they leave school than those who have been educated in the more protective environment of special schools.

The social learning benefits of integrated provision inevitably overlap with the benefits accruing to all pupils, but contribute most particularly to the enhanced dignity of the special needs pupil.

Curricular entitlement

The curricular breadth in a mainstream school will inevitably be greater than that which can be offered in a special school. Thus, in terms of the special needs child's entitlement to a broad and balanced curriculum, a mainstream environment is more likely to fulfil it. This point is probably stronger in the secondary phase, but remains a central benefit at all levels of education.

We have summarized the key arguments in favour of integration and would like to stress the importance of seeing the benefits as being to *all* pupils, to teachers and to society as a whole. It is possible to obscure what are perfectly rational arguments in favour of integration by stating them in over-emotional terms. Naturally this is an emotive area, particularly for parents, and it is therefore all the more necessary for teachers to achieve a dispassionate view.

Arguments against integration

There is undeniably a strong counter-argument in favour of segregated special education; the very continued existence of this provision, as a vibrant part of the general education system, testifies to its perceived value. This healthy continuance is not merely due to the paucity of provision in mainstream schools. Certain parents and older children positively prefer the special sector, and many professionals involved in making formal assessments recommend such placements.

Parental choice

Some parents look to the special sector to provide what they perceive as vital for their child, i.e. protection. While this certainly does not apply to all parents, it is easy to understand why some parents – those with a physically frail child, for example – might feel it to be of top priority. In many cases, parents want anything but a protective atmosphere for their child, seeking instead the challenge and 'rough and tumble' of a mainstream school. There is often more involved than the physical aspects of protection. Parents may also be seeking to protect their child from failure and its negative outcomes. This is often the case with parents who recognize a very real developmental or learning gap between their child and his peers. When older children start to make self-critical comments or complain about always failing and not being 'as good as everybody else', it is possible to appreciate why parents might turn to the special sector in a bid to restore their child's self-image and confidence, and to avoid potential later problems, such as school refusal, truancy and behaviour problems.

Understandably, many parents also wish to protect their special needs child from the perceived threat of the other children. They fear that their child might be the subject of bullying.

In a sense, the motive behind these preferences is to protect their children from the pain of realizing that they are different. Parents with these fears will be attracted to special schools, many of which, particularly at the primary phase, seek to provide a very caring and family-like atmosphere.

Not only are most special schools small, they are often well endowed with equipment and resources as a result of charitable donations. Obviously this will be very attractive to concerned parents, and can outweigh more relevant questions about the type of education on offer at special as opposed to mainstream schools.

This is not to suggest that special schools are largely about providing a cosy, supportive and well-equipped environment. Such a view would be grossly unfair to the quality and professionalism of special school staff. It is really about how parents and some professionals *perceive* the special school sector. It is equally unrealistic to contend that mainstream schools cannot ever offer the levels of personal, emotional and physical protection that certain children require.

The lure of the special

The word 'specialist' is connected with distinct images and attitudes for most of us. *Special* schools are largely staffed by teachers who are *specialists* by virtue of initial or subsequent training and experience. There is undoubtedly real expertise in many special schools, particularly those catering for pupils with severe learning difficulties, physical disabilities, sensory difficulties and language problems. What is not often appreciated, however, is the growing level of expertise and successful experience among mainstream teachers, particularly special needs teachers and co-ordinators. Parents and, indeed, many mainstream teachers who have had little contact with special schools may be led into believing the myth that special needs children will always be better off in a *specialist* environment.

It is undeniable that class sizes are smaller and levels of non-teaching assistance greater in special schools. Thus, the argument that a child attending such a school is bound to receive more attention is difficult to counter, particularly when mainstream class sizes are over 30, with little non-teaching support. Nevertheless, particularly for statemented pupils, it is always worth investigating whether the child could be allocated non-teaching support in a mainstream school before recommending a special school placement. Pupil–adult ratios will not always matter more than the sheer quality of teaching and support offered.

Special schools exist: therefore they should be used

If all special schools were to be closed, the basis of this argument would disappear. Pupils would have to be integrated. Meanwhile the very existence of large numbers of special schools exerts a considerable influence over those who are recommending them to parents. It is a considerable financial and managerial challenge for an LEA to invest additional sums into supporting a child in a mainstream school when there is spare capacity in special schools. (In this context it is worth remembering that the debate over special schools is concerned with Warnock's 2 per cent of the school population; the remaining 18 per cent of the estimated 20 per cent with special educational needs are already integrated.)

Another aspect of the lure of the special is that most parents are likely to be heavily influenced by the advice of the range of *specialists* with whom they will have had contact during the formal assessment of their child. Acknowledging their own inexperience, they feel bound to rely on the advice of such practitioners, and it is the case that many of the specialists recommend special school placements.

There are many reasons why psychologists, doctors, paramedical staff and teachers might advise parents to opt for a special school, ranging from blind prejudice or ignorance to well-balanced advice, based on a realistic knowledge of a child's actual needs and of the levels of support available in the mainstream schools. Whatever the reasons, while so much support is being given to segregated education, the swing towards integration must inevitably be diminished.

The views of the child

Finally there is the argument that the views of the child should be taken into account whenever possible. When decisions are being taken about the most suitable kind of education for a child with special needs, there is always the danger – for professionals and parents – of assuming that they know what is 'best for the child', without ever eliciting the child's view. Both the present authors have encountered special needs children and adults with disabilities who have experienced being placed in mainstream schools and who have hated it. It can happen that a child may *appear* to be successfully integrated, but without establishing the child's real views it is impossible to be sure that this is so. In general terms, the older the pupil, the more weight should be attached to his views. Ultimately, it becomes a question of balancing a difficult equation, but the child's voice should be a key part of that problem.

Weighing up the arguments

Both the defenders and the opponents of integration are vehement, and their vehemence has been fuelled by the impact of the Warnock Report and the 1981 Education Act. It is interesting that in the case of parents, whose views are influential, positions tend to depend on the nature of their particular child's case: thus the parents of Down's syndrome children are often strong advocates of integration, while parents of dyslexic children often seek separate special schools. Parental pressure is hard to resist. LEA officers who support the legislation that promotes integration will find it hard to put this into practical effect in the face of parental opposition.

Financial considerations also play a significant role in determining what kind of provision is deemed 'suitable' for special needs children. Unless money is allocated to mainstream schools so they can provide adequate support for special needs children, they are not likely to be seen – nor to see themselves – as suitable places for such children.

WHERE THEN IS THE PRESSURE FOR INTEGRATION?

The pressure for integration originated from the seminal Warnock report and the resultant Education Act 1981. The Report was researched against the wider context of desegregation being advocated for a variety of groups. Now the government, through the DFE, advocates that, wherever possible, children should be educated in mainstream schools, notwithstanding that adequate funding has not been provided to finance such a major change in practice. Still, the official tide is, overall, moving towards integration, occasionally with more ebb than flow. The rate of change is certainly slower than the advocates of integration originally envisaged. Special schools continue to flourish and there is no indication of their imminent wholesale demise. Nevertheless, special needs pupils in mainstream schools are generally being dealt with in more appropriate and successful ways.

Officially, all LEAs have to be in favour of integration. An education officer, Tom Peryer, has commented:

> There can not be an authority in the country which does not explicitly state that its policy is to integrate children as far as possible into ordinary schools. In some ways it does not matter that the phrase 'as far as possible' can mean all things to all men. The point is that this is now a commonplace of all policy statements. (Baker and Bovair, 1989, p. 214)

Peryer goes on to make the telling statement that all authorities are beginning to be judged by how many special needs pupils are not in special schools. The judges are likely to be inspection teams, politicians, activist groups and parent lobbies.

Whatever the prevailing official view, the move towards integration varies enormously within LEAs. Thus, as Allan Day, a Shropshire headteacher, has observed:

> It is . . . left to individual LEAs, under pressures from local and national ideological, economic, pressure groups and litigious processes to move towards integration in different ways, and choose their own interpretations of the future roles of special schools . . . (Baker and Bovair, 1989, p. 62)

The pressures on authorities will be translated into changes in practice and changes in the expectations placed on schools.

Thus far, schools have varied dramatically in their willingness and capacity to provide for their own special needs pupils and also to accept pupils from the special schools sector. There may be some schools that are motivated to develop special needs provision as a means of improving their image (Hegarty, 1982, p. 104):

> There is a symbolic component as well, the presence of pupils with special needs in a school can imply important statements about the nature of the school, its tolerance for diversity and its regard for individuals.

However, this line of argument is likely to carry weight mainly in the case of pupils with obvious special needs, such as wheelchair-bound pupils or those who wear a hearing aid. The argument does not work so well when applied, for example, to behaviourally disturbed or autistic children. Having children with *these* needs is not likely to enhance the school's image, and schools that favour accepting them are likely to do so for altruistic and idealistic reasons, such as the commitment of the head and governors to creating a tolerant, supportive society.

Why has the pace of integration been relatively slow?

Although historians will probably identify the Education Act 1981 as a key piece of legislation, not only within education but also within the wider sphere of the law concerning people with special needs, they will also regard it as legislation that did not achieve its full intent because of the failure to resource its implementation appropriately. When the Act was introduced, it was argued that major changes in procedures and educational practice could be effected using existing resources. What could have been a dramatic piece of radical legislation became, particularly in regard to the issue of integration, a series of statements indicating the direction in which schools and LEAs were *supposed* to move. The costing implications were never realistically examined at the time when the legislation was introduced. Now, years later and as financial control is increasingly removed from authorities, the issue is revealed even more clearly in its true political colours.

Pilot studies were made on a number of integration schemes throughout the UK for which adequate funding and planning had been provided. These indicated (Hegarty *et al.*, 1981) that children with special needs could be successfully educated in mainstream schools given proper financial provision. However, such findings were not allowed to influence subsequent legislation or budget allocations.

A number of commentators on the national picture, including Bovair (Baker and Bovair, 1989, p. 82), have suggested that:

> a cheap form of integration has occurred, avoiding the cost of special school placement, yet without the necessary resource input in the ordinary setting, all too often at the expense of the population that truly has the right to benefit from the concept.

The necessary 'resource input' should include funding for the appointment of adequate numbers of additional teachers and non-teaching assistants, and the provisions of training. With these benefits would come the precious commodity of time:

Time to make oneself aware of the needs of those with learning and physical handicaps, the time to see to their pastoral needs, the time to create appropriate and adequate materials that would allow access to many of the curriculum areas. Time is money. (Baker and Bovair, 1989, p. 82)

This statement encapsulates many of the frustrations expressed by practitioners, who feel that they have been asked to put into operation a sound idea, but without the resources to do so. It has been argued that switching funding from special schools to mainstream provision would be enough. But special schools cannot be closed overnight. Extra funding is needed to cover the interim situation when increasing numbers of pupils are being supported in mainstream schools but some still remain in the special schools. Thus 'switching resources from the special to the mainstream sector' does not convey a realistic option.

Inadequate funding is not the whole of the problem: attitudes of teachers and governing bodies have also slowed the pace of change. These attitudes are not necessarily borne of unwillingness or outright opposition, but more of a reserve about embarking on major and dramatic change without the necessary training and preparation. Nowadays, when the management of change is hailed as a cornerstone in management support services and is a key part of management consultancy, it is easy to see that the changes expected of schools were not managed effectively at the national (and therefore local) level, leaving little possibility that they would occur. Indeed this makes all the more impressive such improvements as have been achieved in meeting the needs of special needs children already within schools. Equally, it is hardly surprising that relatively few children have left special schools. Such underfunded and weakly managed attempts at making major changes were never going to achieve the initial ambitions of the Warnock Report.

Training of mainstream staff

Some LEAs embarked on programmes of in-service training in the wake of the 1981 Act, recognizing the need to improve the skills of mainstream staff who were to be asked to cope with special needs pupils. However, such provision was patchy and usually insufficient to support staff on a long-term basis. This is part of the scenario of mismanagement: teachers were expected to take on a significant change for which they were inadequately prepared.

Legislation and teacher morale

Teacher morale is clearly a vital factor when it comes to meeting the challenge of integration. As the impact of the 1981 Act began to be felt in schools, towards the latter part of the 1980s, a new wave of major legislative reforms gave teachers more than enough to cope with in the way of change. Inevitably, morale dropped, and with it the willingness and capacity to cope positively with the demands of special needs children.

INTEGRATION TODAY AND THE FUTURE FOR THE MAINSTREAM TEACHER

For those who would wish to see a large-scale reduction in the number of special schools and the switching of resources to support their pupils in mainstream schools, the current situation is not encouraging. There have been various successful integration schemes, but progress has been piecemeal. Hall (1992, p. 21) argues that 'we might justifiably speak of an "integration salad" to describe the bewildering array of activities and organisational forms which are described as "integrated"'.

The progress towards widespread and real integration will probably continue in this fashion, given that there seems to be little political will to pursue the process more vigorously. Indeed, recent legislation may even have a constraining effect (see pp. 142–6).

Nonetheless there is a chance that teachers in a mainstream school may find themselves facing the challenge of teaching a child who hitherto would have gone into a special school from reception age. The way they cope with this challenge will influence the course of future provision. It must be recognized therefore that these additional demands of teachers will necessitate the acquisition and development of a variety of teaching and classroom management skills. For teachers new to the profession, or in training, this challenge poses a significant expectation of their professional practice. The range of pupil needs and abilities with which they will be expected to cope will be extended and may necessitate reshaping personal expectations of what will be required for a particular age group. Teachers' roles and day-to-day working practices may have to be rethought in response to active programmes of integration.

Parental aspirations and demands, even if these are achieved only through resorting to formal appeals, will also be major determiners of school and authority practice. It is also likely that the increasingly well organized support organizations and pressure groups, which operate with sophisticated legal backing, will have some effect on hastening or retarding the process of integration.

Some teachers will be given the opportunity to participate in the integration of special school pupils into mainstream classes on a full-time and permanent basis. It is likely, however, that moves towards the part-time integration of special school pupils will continue. This is all the more likely if special school staff continue to develop a role as outreach support teachers to mainstream colleagues. Teacher traffic in *both* directions would be even more likely to ease the process of partial integration.

As schools continue to assume control over their financial management, it is likely that the process of integration will need to be funded on an individual basis. Schools may well be perfectly willing to accept special school pupils if the latter are accompanied by the necessary levels of funding to ensure a successful placement.

To end on a positive note, it must be recognized that some significant progress has been achieved within mainstream schools in meeting the needs of pupils with special needs. In-house procedures for the identification of special needs pupils, the development of appropriate responses and monitoring systems have all contributed to ensuring better levels of curricular and general integration for those pupils within their own schools. Montgomery (1990) has provided a useful research-based overview of several examples of effective integration for pupils with learning difficulties. In addition, Norwich (1990) has analysed the concept and practice of integration, linking the debate to a discussion of the essential ideas and practical realities. It remains to be seen whether the process can be extended to children at present attending special schools. The next few chapters will provide an overview of the techniques, approaches and procedures which have facilitated these improvements.

CHAPTER SUMMARY

This chapter has provided a general background to integration issues and existing provision. We placed the concept of integration in a wider context and several related issues in other areas of social policy and development have been examined. In looking at the concept of integration, we described the difficulty of defining it in terms of practice. An examination of arguments for and against educating special needs pupils in mainstream schools demonstrated the divergence of views and the size of the challenge which integration presents.

We offered views on why widespread integration has been difficult to achieve and speculated over future developments, ending on an optimistic note by recognizing the real achievements that have occurred in mainstream schools.

SUGGESTIONS FOR FURTHER READING

Association of Educational Psychologists (1989) *Integration: Problems and Possibilities for Change: Report of the Working Party on the Educational Integration of Children and Young People Who Have Special Needs*. Durham: AEP. This is a short and highly readable review of the current situation; it includes recommendations for teachers, LEAs and central government.

Baker, D. and Bovair, K. (1989) *Making the Special Schools Ordinary*, Vol. 1. Lewes: Falmer Press. A stimulating collection of papers by a variety of practitioners, many of which include issues related to the integration debate and the future place of segregated education.

Hegarty, S., Pocklington, K. and Lucas, D. (1981) *Educating Pupils with Special Need in the Ordinary School*. Windsor: Nelson/NFER. A detailed overview of a research project concerning the education of special needs pupils in mainstream settings. This is a book for the enthusiast, but the first chapter is well worth a read in connection with the concept of integration.

Tomlinson, S. (1982) *A Sociology of Special Education*. London: Routledge & Kegan Paul. An authoritative and detailed overview of segregated education from the historical and sociological perspectives.

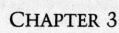

CHAPTER 3

Learning difficulties: terms, principles and teacher power

CHAPTER OVERVIEW

In this chapter, which sets the scene for material of a more practical orientation, we look at attempts to achieve precise and meaningful definitions in this area, including attempts made in the relevant legislation. We go on to propose a more pragmatic and useful set of working guidelines. In the process we address the topic of the mythical 'norm' and point to the importance of context when it comes to defining the needs of individual children.

The most important asset in the classroom is the teacher. We argue here, as elsewhere, that teacher attitudes play a powerful role in formulating a positive response to the challenge of meeting the needs of pupils with learning difficulties. To encourage and support such positive attitudes, we offer a constructive overview of attempts to produce workable definitions and practical guidelines for teaching pupils with specific learning difficulties.

DEFINING OUR TERMS

What is meant by the term 'learning difficulty'?

Each of us will, at many times in our lives, experience learning difficulties with particular subjects, skills or novel situations. The classic modern dilemma seems to be that of the intelligent, educated person who, when first faced with a word processor or computer, displays intense resistance to acquiring the necessary skills. This

23

learning 'problem' seems to persist despite the instruction received from various experts including that person's own children, and the availability of 'user-friendly' manuals.

In this case, are such apparently intelligent people exhibiting a specific learning problem? Is it a question of anxiety or attitude? Is there an interactional problem between the learner and the learning environment in its broadest sense? Is it simply a lack of essential ability or is it a short-term individual learning problem? In this situation it would be inappropriate to identify the individual as having 'learning problems' on the basis of initially poor performance, yet this is what often happens in parallel classroom situations, where such rash judgements lead to children being too readily labelled as having learning problems as a result of a weak start with a new teacher or subject.

It can be illuminating, when trying to conceptualize what we mean by a learning problem, to think back to a recent situation when we found it difficult to learn something; it helps us to realize that the 'problem' is not always within the learner and that we should not assume that certain pupils have difficulty in learning *all* new skills. This is manifestly not so in our own experience. In the authors' case, had the acquisition of foreign languages or the development of musical skills played a greater part in the curriculum of our secondary schools, then one of us would certainly not have been designated 'university material'. And we can each remember pupils who surprised teaching staff by displaying skills that were unexpected because the children had been labelled: 'has a learning problem'. One such 9-year-old had great difficulty with conventional maths, yet he astonished us by his ability to work out complex racing bets; his father was, in fact, a bookmaker.

Here again we encounter a lack of clarity when it comes to concepts related to special needs: the term 'learning problem', like integration, defies clear definition. It, too, is context-based; that is, its real meaning and value depend on the situation(s) in which the term is being applied. Our experience suggests that the lack of clarity is reflected in the relevant legislation and in attempts to interpret it.

Clear, precise and recognizable criteria would be invaluable, hence the lure in past years of intelligence tests. These purported to measure children's intelligence by comparing their test performance with that of an allegedly 'average' child of the same age and thereby producing an intelligence quotient (IQ). Children whose IQ score fell below a designated point were deemed to have all-round learning difficulties or, to use the pre-Warnock terminology, to be educationally sub-normal (moderate): ESN(M). It was believed that intelligence tests measured a child's ability with such accuracy that one could predict how well the youngster would cope with all aspects of the curriculum.

+ *inadequate*

This made the assessment of a child's potential relatively easy; it could be completed in the time it took to administer the test. However, the belief that ability could be measured, and the likely performance of a child assumed, ran counter to reality.

Intelligence tests originally designed for (white) British children have been shown to be of questionable validity and reliability, particularly when given to children from different linguistic and cultural backgrounds. Another, and significant, reason for dispensing with them is that they do not help a teacher to devise a curriculum appropriate to the child's needs. Thus intelligence tests are redundant, practically as well as functionally.

Official attempts at defining the terms

The Education Act 1981 specifies that children have 'special educational needs' if they have 'learning difficulties' which call for 'special educational provision' to be made for them (section 1). Here we find a notable degree of circularity. It would have been helpful if, at this stage, the framers of the legislation had formulated a clear definition of the term 'learning difficulty'. Regrettably, they failed to do so. Pupils are described as having a learning difficulty (section 1.4) if:

> they have a significantly greater difficulty in learning than the majority of children of their age,

and/or

> they have a disability which either prevents or hinders them from making use of educational facilities of a kind generally provided in schools within the area of the local authority concerned for children of their age.

Such a definition is obviously confusing: it relates not only to the child but also to the context in which the child is taught. Moreover it encourages us to imagine there is a 'norm'. The norm is a concept derived, once again, from psychometric approaches. It is based on the view that it is possible to determine in detail what the 'average' child of a particular age group is able to achieve. This belief includes the notion that statistics obtained from selective samples can enable practitioners to make general statements about the 'average' child regardless of socio-economic background, learning opportunities and a host of other relevant variables. Would that it were so! Life, and legislating, would be much simpler.

The mythical 'norm'

The attempt to define learning difficulties by comparison to a 'norm' is not based on reliable data about what 'average' children achieve and, unhelpfully, pushes us into speculative judgements. Even if the norm is defined in terms of the general standards of attainment in a partic- ular school, the notion of 'norm' is still unhelpful if it encourages us to believe that the problem is exclusively *within* the child. Move him to another school where, for whatever reasons, the overall standards are notably lower and the 'learning problem', so defined, disappears! One school's 'learning problem' child could be another school's 'average achiever' and vice versa. Every school, and every class within a school, will have pupils who exhibit comparative learning diffi- culties. Thus it may be more helpful to refer to the size of the gap be- tween such children and the majority of their classmates.

A pragmatic approach to definitions?

Where does all of this lead us in terms of helping teachers meet the needs of pupils whose progress in learning is markedly behind that of their peer group? To repeat, we need to be cautious about assigning prescriptive labels (with the related danger of issuing self-fulfilling prophecies). If we recognize that special educational needs partly result from unmet curricular and teaching needs, then we have a possible approach to defining learning difficulties: a child could be described as having or exhibiting learning difficulties as a result of inappropriate curriculum differentiation and insufficiently adapted teaching. This view lay behind Dessent's (1987, p. 7) comment:

> If the learning environment is 'sympathetic' and geared towards meeting individual needs, there will be few special educational needs.

This view should be borne in mind when considering how best to define learning difficulties.

But I know what I mean by a child with learning difficulties

Ironically, having said all that, we must admit that most teachers feel able to describe *what they mean* by a child with learning problems. Most of us would be able to think of a past pupil for whom such a descriptive term would have been accurate. As Wolfendale (1988, p. 4) pointed out, 'we are constrained by our basic human tendency to group and classify all manner of phenomena, including children in our charge'.

Stereotyping has its uses as well as its dangers. As long as we are aware of the latter, there is value in outlining those general features or behaviours which lead us to describe children as having learning difficulties. Solity and Bull (1987, p. 8), attempting to offer a general description of pupils who are falling behind their peers, wrote:

> in short, certain children present us with difficulties, because they are
> behind their peers on the curriculum, are not making satisfactory progress,
> lack concentration and have lost interest in work.

It would be surprising if readers failed to recognize this description. In our experience, such children sometimes also exhibit very
low self-esteem, feel that they and their efforts are not valued and
view school as a largely unrewarding experience. To affirm the
legitimacy of these observations, we would ask readers to think back
to their own experiences of learning failures at school and to analyse
their emotional reactions. The essential point is, however, that this
is a *general* description, and we should approach each child as an
individual and not to expect a complete 'set' of characteristics for
every pupil exhibiting some degree of learning difficulty.

In all classes there will be children who learn more slowly than
their peer group in most subject areas. There will also be children
who have problems with particular aspects of the curriculum or
specific skills. Ultimately, we may have to accept that there are
no clearly defined procedures for deciding whether a pupil has a
'learning problem'. It is a situation-specific phenomenon. To adopt a
functional approach, it may be useful to accept that teachers should
be the ones to consider the appropriateness and relevance of the
term 'learning difficulty' within the context of their classroom. If the
teacher recognizes the need to modify the curriculum content, to
adapt teaching styles or to rethink her whole strategy, this will, it
is to be hoped, be in direct response to the recognition of children's
needs – of their 'learning problems'. Teachers are more likely to
pursue such approaches if the learning gap between the child and the
larger body of the class is considerable. Often it is possible to identify
a group of such pupils in a given class.

It is advisable to be cautious in assigning labels to children. Teachers
should accept that the response, 'Well, it really depends on the circumstances in your classroom' is not an excuse for a lack of precision,
but a realistic view of the situation. One can begin to appreciate the
apparent circularity of the attempts at producing official definitions
in this area. A functional approach does not accept that there are
simple objective measures which provide the factual basis for deciding on whether a child has a learning problem: it very much depends
on the extent to which the child's difficulties can be accommodated by the curriculum and teaching style within the classroom.

The pupil with a learning difficulty

We need to look further than a 'within-child' approach which leads us to describe a pupil as 'having a learning problem', in much the same way as we might describe the child as 'having a pronounced squint of the left eye'. The term is more meaningful if we look at the context in which the child is being taught and being expected to learn, and at teacher values and expectations. It is more productive to see a child's special educational needs in terms of how well they are being met by the curriculum and teaching approaches being adopted.

All of this is not to deny that there will inevitably be children for whom it would be ridiculous to avoid the use of the term. In such a case, to pretend otherwise and not to take appropriate action would be against the child's better interests. For certain situations this may mean that the child's needs can be best met in a special school or unit attached to a mainstream school.

The process by which such decisions are reached has been determined by the Education Act 1981. There is a specified procedure, usually referred to as a section 5 assessment. Parents, teachers, the school doctor and the educational psychologist all contribute to this assessment. If it is felt that the child's special educational needs can only be met by provision not normally available to all pupils, then the child is issued with a Statement of Special Educational Needs. (For further information on this, see Chapter 9, or Solity and Raybould, 1988.)

The Education Act 1981

This important Act, which was implemented in 1983, introduced into legislation many of the recommendations from the radical Warnock Report (1978), *Special Educational Needs*. It sought to enhance the rights of individual children with special needs within the education system. This was reflected pointedly in the changes in terminology, from the somewhat derogatory labels previously applied to children to descriptive categories of need. Secondly, the Act introduced clearly defined identification and assessment procedures, by which

parental rights were massively strengthened. Clear procedures were determined which *could* lead to some children
being issued with a Statement of Special Educational Need.
The major weakness of this legislation was that it was not
funded separately and LEAs were expected to finance special
needs provision from their existing resources. The degree to
which the Act has been implemented has varied considerably
across authorities (Goacher *et al.*, 1988).

However, the vast majority of pupils with learning problems are
and should be educated in neighbourhood schools alongside their
friends. Formal assessments are unnecessary for most such children.
Ultimately, it is teachers who must face the challenge of acting on
their assessments to help those children in their class who display
varying degrees of learning difficulties. Even if these difficulties are
relative, manifesting themselves only in the context of that particular
classroom, they still represent a reality calling for adapted teaching
methods and adapted curriculum content. We do not feel that teachers
are particularly helped in identifying such children with the use of
screening procedures or Standard Assessment Tasks (SATs). In our
experience, teachers are generally very skilled at identifying such
children on the basis of observation and analysis of the child's performance. The real challenge therefore is to know how to respond most
effectively having identified the problem.

KEY PRINCIPLES AND IMPLICATIONS FOR TEACHERS

It is a *myth* that there is any such thing as a distinct and separate set
of teaching skills in special needs education. The principles which
underpin good classroom teaching are the very same as those which
will enable teachers to cope with children experiencing learning
difficulties. There is a need to analyse the teaching processes more
thoroughly and certainly to look at the teaching outcomes in more
detail. In the process of challenging and examining teaching styles
for such pupils, we will undoubtedly improve teaching for *all*
children.

There is a fear associated with this whole area which we refer to
as 'expertosis': the fear that to be successful, the teacher has to be an
expert and to use highly specialist technical equipment and approaches.
Another form of the condition rests on the belief that good special
needs teaching only takes place in the rarefied atmosphere of special

schools or units where teachers are currently paid more than mainstream colleagues.

In our experience, mainstream teachers can develop their skills and feel more able to cope with such teaching challenges once they have experimented, tried out their ideas, listened critically to other practitioners and honestly evaluated the outcomes. This does not mean that considerable age is an essential prerequisite for excellence in special needs. It may mean, however, that the term 'expert' can be usefully unpacked along these lines.

Much excellent teaching does undeniably go on in special schools. Indeed, we would strongly urge new teachers to visit their local special schools and seek advice and ideas on particular problems, approaches and practical solutions. A well-established link between mainstream and special schools can be a mutually beneficial arrangement for all staff involved. As more and more special schools are proving, their approaches can be readily transposed to the mainstream setting, and adapted productively. Traffic in the reverse direction can be equally beneficial.

The challenge for the mainstream teacher is to produce a curriculum which is adaptive to the needs and strengths of individual children and can also allow for their particular interests and attitudes (Ainscow and Tweddle, 1988). The orientation required is child-centred, i.e. looking upon children as individual learners. We will need to unpick the outcomes of such rhetoric at a later stage. At this point, we would comment that it is necessary for a teacher to be aware of how her personal philosophy relates to such teaching. As Dessent (1987) has claimed, such a personal orientation is a reflection of the teacher's own values, and also perhaps (we would add) the value system operating in the school as a whole, led by the headteacher and governing body.

Good special needs teaching is the ultimate extension of mixed-ability teaching, aiming to remove the need for segregationalist approaches even in a single classroom. Jones (1985) claims that to do so is to extend the concept of normality to cover children with learning difficulties, and the same message is to be found in a wide variety of texts. How realistic an aim it can be for the individual teacher is a moot point. At least, though, it can be a guiding principle for teachers and governing bodies.

There is an implicit danger that, in trying to meet the individual needs of particular learners, the teacher is also likely to single out such children in their own eyes or in the eyes of their peers: the labelling dilemma reappears (Wolfendale, 1987). To achieve good practice in this area will, therefore, not be easy; yet more proof that teaching is not, despite popular belief, an easy profession. How best to offer an appropriate and challenging learning environment to all

30

pupils ensuring that, in particular, pupils with learning difficulties make progress is one of the central issues of contemporary teaching.

THE POWER OF THE TEACHER AND OF TEACHER ATTITUDES

The literature of the psychology of teaching is full of references to the importance of attitude. A positive and practical attitude, one that acknowledges and rewards endeavour, is an essential ingredient in the recipe for success. We all respond to teachers who are encouraging, who notice and reward effort, who seem to take a personal interest in us, who recognize our problems and difficulties yet seem to find ways of working around them and, most importantly, make us feel good about ourselves. All of these skills originate from an essentially positive set of attitudes on the part of the teacher.

Creating a positive set of teacher attitudes

Ironically, such an important 'starter for ten' can be established from the outset even by a new teacher, regardless of experience and practical skills. By adopting good attitudes at the outset, a teacher creates a mental set which will shape her practice. Such a set will percolate through to the children and influence how they approach their own problems.

The process of establishing a positive approach varies with individuals. In our experience, the following can be useful:

Accept and then aim to tackle the issue that coping with the challenges of such pupils will not be easy and, indeed, is not easy even for experienced practitioners.

Recognize that there is a fear element in being personally challenged to meet the needs of these children. This can be born of self-doubt or inexperience of working with people who find learning difficult and who therefore make significant demands on teachers' skills.

Accept that slow-learning children learn slowly! Progress should be viewed as being relative to the individual; forget the unhelpful concept of open and public competition between children.

Accept that there is a need to experiment and in the process experience both success and failure; the only real difficulty arises if we do not learn from both outcomes.

How we as teachers relate to a child is a highly significant ingredient of success. This includes how we talk to the pupil, our body

31

language, our facial expressions and how we respond when the child achieves and fails. Good teachers are often good actors, at least in the classroom. One needs to find a way into this particular part.

It is necessary to learn from other practitioners and to discuss how they achieved success and what failures they experienced.

If nobody else is prepared to do it, teachers should praise and reward themselves by recognizing their own achievements and progress with individual children and groups.

Attitudes are very much a part of individual make-up and orientation. In some cases they are bound up with choosing to be a teacher. They are difficult to change. Nevertheless, we would strongly argue that new practitioners should give themselves some thinking time to sort through their own viewpoints, to recognize their fears and apprehensions in a pro-active way, rather than trying to cope in a purely reactive fashion.

Day-to-day work

In the process of working with children with learning difficulties, teachers will find it hard not to build a particularly close relationship, and they can experience a great personal 'buzz' in celebrating success with a child who has struggled to achieve a particular skill. There is an additional gain in this, as Croll and Moses (1985) (quoted in Dessent (1987, p. 164)) have been able to conclude: 'Teachers' attitudes towards children with special needs become altogether more positive and optimistic as a result of experiencing success with such children.'

This personalized approach will enable practitioners to tune into the idiosyncrasies of their pupils. Thus, for example, some pupils may rejoice in open and loud praise from their teacher, others may cringe at the prospect. Some children hate being touched by teachers, whereas an occasional hug can be the most powerful of rewards to others. Children vary in their responses to teaching strategies: games can be anathema to some children, the computer the nearest thing to Nirvana; some children learn best by imitation, others by guided help at completing the tasks and so on. It is valuable to find out such facts about these pupils in particular, but also to recognize that such reactions change as pupils change and mature.

It is known that linking meaningful rewards to learning can greatly improve the chances that what has been learnt will be retained and that the child will want to learn more. The approach to the relationship cannot be simplistic; however, it is not enough to shower praise around like confetti. We know that the experience of receiving rewards creates a more positive attitude on the part of the recipient. Likewise it is pleasanter to reward than to punish children. Research evidence would seem to indicate that to be most effective, rewards should be used sparingly but well: the pupil must learn that to earn the praise requires hard work but is really worth it. An atmosphere can thereby be created in the class or group in which positive encouragement and appropriate praise give rise to the confidence necessary for pupils to face new tasks and activities. In short, the positive classroom reflecting a supportive and positive relationship between teacher and pupil is one in which success and improvements are more likely for all pupils and particularly for those experiencing learning problems.

PUPILS WHO EXHIBIT SPECIFIC LEARNING DIFFICULTIES

Analysing the label

The term 'dyslexia' will inevitably feature in any discussion about children with learning difficulties. The popular view of such children is that they are generally and certainly verbally bright, but that they have specific learning difficulties over reading or writing, or both. Thus a pupil may have extreme problems in learning to read, to spell, to write or a combination of these and yet the same child will be perfectly capable in number work, oral skills and other aspects of the curriculum. Such children therefore tend to stand out, to surprise teachers because of the quite specific nature of their learning problems.

There is, to say the least, a wide divergence of views about many aspects of this issue, including how such pupils should be assessed or their needs specified, how the 'condition' should be overcome, which teaching strategies are appropriate, where teaching should take place and who should carry it out. It is an emotive issue, particularly for parents seeking an explanation and help for their child. It has also become a political (though not party political) issue as debates about the availability of resources, attitudes to such children, the supposed aetiology of the problem and the inevitable proliferation of experts create more hot air and little by way of productive help for children and their teachers. There is a semi-medicalized model which underpins some of the belief systems that abound in this area. In a sense, parents are searching for a label that will distinguish their child from the pupils who have more pervasive learning problems and who are therefore considered to be generally less intelligent. Indeed, such belief systems are supported by the use of intelligence tests to identify the fact that there is a marked disparity between the child's score on the two aspects of such tests: the verbal and the performance or non-verbal. Such children are often 'diagnosed' as being of average or, more usually, above average intelligence but as having specific learning difficulties. *tests* Whether any of this is of practical use to the teacher is extremely debatable. The teacher does have to recognize the enigma of such pupils: although they do exhibit problems in some areas, they also display considerable capabilities in others. The challenge is to make the most of the latter rather allowing the former to dominate the child's whole life.

A pragmatic approach

This book is not an appropriate forum in which to deal with all of the above issues; rather we aim to formulate a practical approach for teachers. Such children can and should be taught in mainstream classes by mainstream teachers. The approaches described in the next chapter can be used profitably, but should be geared specifically to those curriculum and skill areas in which the pupil experiences difficulties. Various texts have been written by experienced practitioners outlining the apparently different ways of teaching children with specific learning difficulties. These are certainly a valuable source of ideas, approaches, materials and working strategies. Ironically, however, there is little to distinguish these approaches from the techniques adopted and developed by experienced teachers of special needs pupils. Reciprocally, the approaches advocated by dyslexia 'specialists' can be used by teachers working with pupils exhibiting more general learning difficulties.

A more pragmatic approach is to regard learning problems as existing on a dimension even within one classroom. The nature of a child's difficulties determines their needs and thus how the teacher attempts to meet those needs. The pupil with specific difficulties requires specific help which can be provided as part of the teaching routines within the classroom.

Teachers need to bear in mind that pupils have distinct strengths in other areas of the curriculum which can be utilized when planning an overall curriculum. The high anxiety levels often linked with such children need to be addressed positively. Particular emphasis can be placed on including the pupil in determining what has to be learnt and why. Wherever possible, the child should be involved in the monitoring of progress; gains should be celebrated, but in a manner appropriate to the child's personality. A key requirement seems to be the need to achieve a determination on behalf of the pupil to continue to make and to recognize progress, rather than viewing his condition as a harbinger of failure. Once again, the teachers concerned need to recognize the possibility of success. They can make significant contributions to the child's progress; this area is not the realm of the specialist into which 'ordinary' teachers wander at their peril.

CHAPTER SUMMARY

In attempting to steer a tricky course through the complex and sometimes seemingly circular definitions relating to children with learning difficulties, we analysed the official approach before outlining a pragmatic one. We argued that, in practice, teachers have usually developed a clear picture of how children with such difficulties present in the classroom, and we find little of value in the concept of the 'norm'.

In translating key principles into workable implications for teachers, we debunked the notion that mainstream teachers need to acquire a wholly new and separate set of skills. We did, however, highlight the centrality of teacher attitudes in creating a positive set towards the challenge of teaching such children.

Finally, the thorny issue of pupils who exhibit specific learning difficulties was briefly discussed, including the political implications of the debate. We argued that such pupils should be taught in a mainstream environment but that their needs should be approached on an individual level recognizing strengths and emotional difficulties.

The overall thrust of the chapter was to persuade the reader that this whole area, though not easy, is one which can and should be tackled by all teachers. The key principles lie in the need to learn from fellow practitioners, to analyse one's own practice honestly and to avoid being put off the whole area by myths and unnecessarily confused attempts to achieve meaningful definitions.

SUGGESTIONS FOR FURTHER READING

Ainscow, M. and Tweddle, D. (1988) *Encouraging Classroom Success*. London: Fulton Press. A readable book which represents the authors' reappraisal of their earlier arguments related to the use of curriculum objectives in the light of experience. The concepts surrounding special needs are well addressed, leading to thoughtful practical suggestions.

Dessent, T. (1988) *Making the Ordinary School Special*. Basingstoke: Falmer. A well argued, somewhat weightier book which takes the key concepts and provides rationales and approaches to support the integration of special needs children in mainstream schools.

Pearson, L. and Lindsay, G. (1986) *Special Needs in the Primary School*. Exeter: NFER/Nelson. A broad-based overview of the 1981 Education Act, leading to a framework for approaching special needs in general together with suggestions regarding practical approaches.

Solity, J. E and Raybould, E. (1988) *A Teacher's Guide to Special Needs: A Positive Response to the 1981 Act.* Milton Keynes: Open University Press. A workshop manual approach to the details of the procedures arising from the Act. The text is supplemented by explanations of key issues and related practice. Chapters 1 and 2 would be particularly valuable at this stage.

CHAPTER 4

Learning difficulties and curriculum differentiation: procedures and practical approaches

CHAPTER OVERVIEW

In this chapter we will look at a number of key factors that should be considered by teachers in mainstream classrooms, including detailed adaptations to the curriculum, the use of objectives, the value of the assessment-through-teaching model and the importance of teachers as a resource in themselves. We will then go on to look at classroom organization, pupil involvement, collaborative teaching and, briefly, parental involvement.

A note of caution: treating such factors as if they were discrete aspects is misleading, although convenient for the purpose of discussion. The overall organization and management of teaching remains complex and should not be regarded as a series of discrete aspects to be addressed in isolation.

THE CURRICULUM

The advent of the National Curriculum brought with it a massive concentration on what should be taught in English and Welsh schools. In order to accommodate the demands of the numerous folders and commentaries, teachers turned to cross-curricular and thematic approaches. The question soon arose of how to adapt the curriculum content and activities for pupils with learning difficulties. Relatively little has been received on this subject from official sources, with the possible exceptions of the National Curriculum Council's circular no. 5, *Implementing the National Curriculum: Participation by*

Pupils with Special Educational Needs (1989a), which was expanded into a report, *A Curriculum for All: Special Educational Needs in the National Curriculum* (1989b), by the Task Group for Special Needs.

The latter document attempts to demonstrate how a range of special needs pupils, including those with learning difficulties, can be given *access to the curriculum* (a key phrase in this area) by adapting schemes of work and using appropriate teaching and curriculum planning strategies. The document is generalist, although it does include practical examples in Maths, English and Science. As with our own approach, the authors aimed to present a number of issues, approaches and views in a way that would allow individual teachers to select the ideas best suited to their needs. It is only through experimentation and through co-operative evaluation that teachers can identify what works for them and for their pupils.

In the search for practical ideas and approaches, teachers will find the Task Group report a useful starting point. Concrete examples and guidelines certainly assist the translation of ideas into teaching methods. In the relatively recent past an almost prescriptive practical approach did much to assist teachers to define, in precise terms, what they needed to teach pupils with learning difficulties. We want to suggest that this once popular approach of using objectives may still provide valuable practical ideas to teachers.

As with many innovations in teaching methods, the objectives approach enjoyed a period of being highly fashionable, but suffered from over-enthusiasm and a lack of critical awareness among some of its advocates. Inevitably, a debunking reaction set in, after which a revised consensus concerning teaching using objectives became established. At least, this is a reflection of what went on in the literature; how the use of teaching to objectives fared in day-to-day classroom situations with ordinary teachers is a different story. Fashionable or not, aspects of the objectives approach had and still have much to offer teachers who wish to give effective help to pupils with learning problems.

The use of behavioural objectives

The value of using defined teaching objectives (Ainscow and Tweddle, 1979, 1984) is that it gives teachers a way to specify, in detailed terms, exactly what they are trying to teach a child, together with criteria for assessing when that particular skill has been learnt.

The approach was adopted with enthusiasm in many special schools. Curriculum areas were broadly and somewhat crudely analysed into a sequence of such objectives; indeed, numerous special schools built the whole curricular structure around these principles. (For a detailed description of the procedures see Solity and Bull, 1987,

Ch. 6; and for a review of the development of the approach, see Norwich, 1990.)

What is a behavioural objective?

A behavioural objective is a clear statement of what it is that the teacher intends the child to learn; it does not include a description of how the teacher intends to teach that skill. Teaching is intended to bring about learning; before we can say that we have taught something successfully, we need to state exactly what we wish our pupils to learn. Objectives are thus clear definitions of intended teaching outcomes that should include:

- A clear description of what the pupil must actually and observably do, *expressed as a verb*
- A *description of the conditions* or circumstances in which the child will be expected to perform the skill
- Criteria for stating *how well the skill must be performed* before it can be stated that successful teaching and learning has taken place

An example of a Sight Word Reading objective would be:

- Child will read orally ten sight words when presented on flash cards to a success rate of 90 percent on two successive occasions.

An example of a number objective would be:

- Child will successfully calculate 8 out of 10 double-digit additions, presented in a written form, on three successive days.

The 'Task Analytical model', which provided a way to break objectives down into a series of smaller teaching steps, became popular. It provided guidance on how to take the slow-learning child progressively and successfully through steps on the way to the full objective. Many structured learning programmes were based on this approach and it has been adapted for most areas of the academic curriculum. One of its key features was the inclusion of regular cycles of repetition and review to reinforce what had been learnt. The aim was to enable the child to progress but at a rate which ensured the retention of learnt material and prevented the child from being asked to learn skills without having already achieved the essential sub-skills.

The place of objectives in the broader curriculum

A teaching programme based entirely on such an approach would be dull and restrictive for both the teacher and the child, and it was accusations of dullness and rigidity of curricular structure that constituted the main criticism against the wholesale use of objectives. Opponents claimed that the rigid and static nature of an objectives curriculum would defeat its purpose of encouraging effective learning because children do not always learn in such a linear fashion. The typical assumption of such critics was that the whole teaching day would be based on achieving listed objectives at the expense of creative activities and opportunities to learn by exploration and group work. It was alleged that the approach dictated a major emphasis on repetitive and mindless rote learning, and argued that the teaching styles would reflect the assumed structure and therefore be unimaginative, prescribed and totally controlled. There was also the allegation that the pupil could become isolated in a curricular sense.

In reality, objectives never did have, and were never intended to have, such a degree of exclusive prominence in curricular or individual programme design. Much of this counter-movement thus consisted of erecting and destroying 'straw men'.

The effect of the criticism was to promote a modified orthodoxy of teaching by objectives (e.g. Ainscow and Tweddle, 1988), which sought to give objectives a more realistic role in the design of curricular structures and teaching methods. Curriculum objectives were designed to provide a skeleton on which the body of the whole teaching environment could be built. They provide the teacher with a structured framework, especially useful for work with individual pupils. The approach encourages teachers to analyse the component skills necessary to achieve mastery of the key skills enumerated in the curriculum. If used sensibly, the model is not restrictive and allows scope for individuality: the broad curriculum content and the teaching styles to be adopted remain in the province of the teacher's discretion. One of the main advantages of the approach lies in its enabling teachers to match the learning task to the pupil's level of attainment, and providing a basis for continual monitoring of progress.

Objectives and the National Curriculum

There is still a place for such an approach in the repertory of teaching skills and the management of learning. When it comes to planning and evaluating specific teaching programmes for achieving Attainment Targets within the National Curriculum, the objectives approach can be of help in the following ways:

- Assisting teachers to separate out and define some parts of what they are trying to teach amidst the sometimes vaguely determined targets of the National Curriculum. Here the practice of describing a teaching outcome as observable pupil behaviour is a useful discipline, and will help teachers to decide not only *where* they are going, but also *when* they arrive at the destination.
- Assisting with overall planning. The objectives approach provides a structure, particularly in a situation where teachers are working in a team.
- Assisting with the on-going evaluation of individual pupils' progress – progress that can be measured by reference to the objectives.

It is interesting to note, incidentally, that the objectives format has been used in the recent recommendations for teacher-based assessment strategies within the National Curriculum. Teachers are encouraged to use activity-based measures as the means of carrying out their ongoing assessments. The *performance* element of how the child responds to the task is intended to assist the teacher to decide whether a child is working at level 1, 2, 3 or 4. For each identified *statement of attainment* teachers have been provided with examples of *evidence of attainment*. Added to this is *advice on setting up particular tasks*. Thus we find all the components of the classic behavioural objective, albeit in a somewhat different framework.

Objectives in practice

A teacher adopting a thematic approach to the teaching of parts of the National Curriculum will need ways to encompass a range of different Attainment Targets from different subject areas. Indeed, within the context of a spread of ability and attainments in a primary classroom, it is quite possible to include work at a number of levels. If the class includes a child or children experiencing learning difficulties, it may be helpful to identify some of the key objectives involved in those Attainment Targets and teach to those particular objectives. This will enable the child to participate in the activities designed to cover the spread of targets. In the case of a child with particular difficulties, the teacher may decide to break the objective down into smaller components and to teach to these, always of course reinforcing the learning with suitable activities over an extended period. If objective-determined activities are included as part of the class day for such pupils, there is likely to be greater success with the objectives and thus with the Attainment Targets. This way of teasing out some of the key objectives and working towards them for part of the contact time with the child or group will allow them to participate with some success in the National Curriculum.

We trust that the reader has noticed our careful use of words in this section and, in particular, the tentative style of our recommendations. Gone, we hope, are the days when commentators in the field wrote with zeal about what teachers ought to do. We are suggesting that there is much to be gained from looking to objectives; they are not, nor should they have ever been described as, *the* answer. Furthermore, as with any method, objectives must be the servant, not the master, of the teacher. They should be as flexible as possible, reviewed regularly and written in a format which is apt for the particular group of teachers using them. Our views can be summarized by this quote from Ainscow and Tweddle (1988, p. 33):

> The way in which objectives should be stated, the degree of specificity that is necessary and how objectives relate to one another are all matters of teacher judgement. There are no rules: objectives are good objectives if they help you and your pupils to succeed.

ASSESSMENT THROUGH TEACHING

In response to the question of how well a particular child in a class group is progressing, the teacher can consider these, among other, factors:

- the written work produced,
- the reading skills demonstrated,
- the child's verbal contributions to discussions, group work and dialogue with the teacher,
- the child's performance on class tests or mini-tests, often ones devised by the teacher.

For the child with learning difficulties, however, the latter source of information will be redundant if the tests are not geared to the child's level of functioning. Imagine, as an adult, being a novice piano student working away at scales but then being 'assessed' on a performance of a Bach fugue. The performance would be unrecognizable, would be an unpleasant experience for the student, and would provide little by way of valuable data and information for the teacher. It would be far more appropriate to assess the pupil on what he is practising and/or on a piece at his level of performance. The situation in the classroom is not dissimilar.

In essence, the link between teaching and assessment should be a close one if it is to ensure that the child is actually making progress in response to the teaching and learning situations being provided. Regular mini-tests to check whether the child has acquired or retained a particular skill or piece of information are far more useful than the end-of-term test or the child's score on a standardized test of attainment.

This approach obviously links up with the use of objectives to determine, at least partially, what a child is trying to achieve. The National Curriculum, it is claimed, specifies what should be taught to children and, roughly, in what order. So far, though, the reality does not entirely measure up to the claim; there is considerable room, indeed need, for interpretation, particularly when teaching children with learning problems.

An assessment-through-teaching model

This can be represented simply in a diagram:

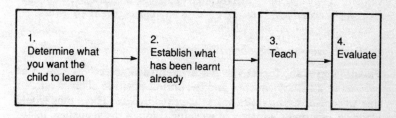

Let us expand on these aspects of the model.

1. Determine what you want the child to learn

Let us expand on these aspects of the model. The first task, seemingly the easiest, is probably the most difficult. Embedded within the National Curriculum are significant but 'fuzzy' words (i.e. words which are difficult to define precisely). Psychologists have pointed out that 'fuzzies' tend to occur when describing behaviour which is open to individual interpretation. We all have a clear picture of what 'cutting paper with scissors' means, but we would probably impose different interpretations on 'shows a willingness to learn'. Fuzzy-spotting can be used to encourage practitioners to be more precise and thereby avoid confusion. The following are all fuzzies: appreciate; awareness of; show signs of a developing interest. Differing interpretations are possible, indeed inevitable. This, together with the complexities produced by the cross-curricular approach, leaves the teacher with a myriad of possible skills that she could teach directly or expect pupils to acquire in the learning situations she has set up.

The task for the teacher faced with a pupil experiencing learning difficulties is to identify the key skills or concepts which that child needs to develop in order to cope most effectively with a particular section of the curriculum or with a chosen scheme of work. This is the kernel of the individualized approach and is based on the teacher's knowledge of that child and the child's needs in the light of the schemes of work being addressed. Basic literacy and numeracy skills would usually feature, but so might language skills or aspects of social skills, such as turn-taking. The teacher has to devise an individualized curriculum from within the National Curriculum; one that is flexible, broad-based, balanced and, whenever possible, takes account of the child's particular strengths. Yet this personalized package should not be regarded as the only learning outcomes possible from the range of activities and teaching presented. Pupils learn a great deal incidentally, sometimes from imitating other children and often by teaching themselves as a result of well-organized teaching and learning opportunities. They can also learn through experiences, through finding out facts for themselves, through making and correcting their errors.

2. *Establish what has been learnt already*

Purists would argue that the list of identified objectives should be ordered in a linear sequence and the child's position charted on that line, according to the skills he has acquired to date. Then, they would claim, it is 'simply' a matter of working through the sequence. In our experience, children, particularly those with learning difficulties, are rarely so amenable. Any attempt at a teaching sequence should be regarded as a flexible guideline only. The main benefit of such a format may be that it helps those producing it to sort out exactly what they will be trying to teach the pupils. In other words, it can be a useful discipline and should not be dismissed.

Initially, teachers find it useful to check their knowledge of the child's skills against the full teaching sequence, and even to test out particular skills, when they are not confident of the child's knowledge. A broad pattern of strengths and weaknesses is thus established. Where one still leads directly into another, it is obviously necessary to tackle them in that order. The sequence should not, however, become a prescriptive or restrictive framework. Movement throughout the sequence should be determined by the pupil's interests, the natural development of a topic, teaching opportunities and the teacher's decisions based on the child's progress.

From time to time, there will be a need to take stock, and generally this analysis of the pupils' progress will identify the targets remaining for teaching. Some skills will need to be approached in a finely grained manner with the broad objectives being broken down into smaller steps. This does seem to be where sticking to a fairly rigid sequence is beneficial. Lastly, it is important to remember that once learnt does not mean forever retained. Skills must be revisited to reinforce the pupil's learning and sometimes to start all over again with a different teaching approach.

3. Teach

How skills are taught is the very essence of pedagogic skills. This is where teachers should draw on their creativity and, most important, learn from one another. New teachers should be encouraged to ask questions, however basic, of more experienced colleagues and to share in the expertise which has been built upon the valuable process of trial and error. Sadly, it is our experience that teachers rarely discuss in detail with colleagues how they actually practise their profession. Wheels are perpetually being reinvented, sometimes within the same school, as teachers strive to cope on their own with teaching children with learning difficulties. Many INSET providers have remarked that one of the most fertile sources of straightforward teaching ideas is to set up task-orientated groups of practising teachers and ask them to solve a teaching problem. For the recently trained teacher, this will not be a novel experience as it is a method often used in teaching practice work. We believe that this can be a valuable in-service approach, particularly in regard to work with special needs pupils.

One good effect of the National Curriculum has been the encouragement it gives teachers to share their experience with colleagues as they try to decide how best to cope with its demands. This sharing is crucially important in the special needs field and, in many schools, has been facilitated by the work of special needs co-ordinators, who have seen their main role as developing such collaborative work. Schools are building up resource banks of ideas, teaching materials, teaching approaches and activities. LEA specialist support teachers and indeed teachers in special schools can be invaluable sources of inspiration, ideas, packages and materials together with liaison links with teachers in other schools. Schools that have welcomed the concept of teacher self-support groups, as advocated in the recommendations of the Elton Report, *Discipline in Schools*, have extended the ideas by incorporating issues relating to special needs. In this way teachers gradually build a repertoire of approaches which work for *them* in the sense that they suit their natural style and achieve progress with most children.

4. Evaluate

The last box in the sequence is particularly demanding in the case of pupils with learning problems. Evaluation is about asking the key question: Is the pupil making progress satisfactorily? If not, the skills may have to be broken down into smaller sub-skills and taught directly. In addition, the teaching processes must be critically examined to see if they can be improved. Ultimately, 'the proof is in the pudding', which, in this case, is pupil achievement. The process of assessment through teaching is cyclical, enabling practitioners to evaluate the effectiveness of their teaching and in the process to define a child's skill levels. In ideal circumstances, assessment through teaching 'is a process which attempts to identify those aspects of the classroom which most effectively promote a child's learning' (Solity and Raybould, 1988, p. 80).

It would be unrealistic to pretend that teachers could evaluate all aspects of their teaching in this stringent way. It is possible, however, to use the process for parts of the curriculum that are causing particular difficulties for an individual child or group of children. Detailed record keeping is necessary in this, to help the teacher describe and analyse a child's progress productively.

The assessment-through-teaching approach in action: an example

Callum, a Year 3 pupil, was clearly experiencing difficulties in acquiring basic reading skills. By comparison with his age peers, he was considerably behind in reading and the gap seemed to be widening at an alarming rate. Normative testing confirmed this but otherwise offered little more information than his teacher and Callum already had.

To date, Callum's teacher had used a variety of the teaching methods which had succeeded with his classmates, including 'look and say' or whole-word approaches allied to a reading scheme, some phonic work and 'reading for meaning' approaches. Reading in this school was very much regarded as a cross-curricular issue and there was a degree of parental involvement. Callum's sight vocabulary was improving, albeit somewhat slowly, but he had real problems in decoding new words. His teacher, therefore, with the help of a specialist support teacher, decided to work on his phonic skills. She felt that he had learnt most of the single-letter sounds and elected to work on final blends using this model.

Step 1: Determine what you want the child to learn. Callum's teacher listed all the main final blends and produced a sequence of phonically regular simple words that included the final blends.

Step 2: Establish what has been learnt already. She set about testing him on the words in her list and compared the results with her observation of his general reading. In fact, she discovered that he had great difficulty with the task, making a worrying range of mistakes with both blends and single-letter sounds. She decided to move backwards and, over a couple of days, tested him on single-letter sounds. She discovered that he needed to learn 14 letter sounds.

Step 3: Teach. As was her usual practice, she decided to teach two quite different-sounding letters at the same time. She used a variety of approaches, presenting the letters in spelling activities, finger-tracing and straightforward letter recognition.

Step 4: Evaluate. After a week's work, Callum's teacher was pleased that he had learnt the two letters and that he could incorporate them into new words.

Repeating the sequence. Intent upon capitalizing on this success, she moved on to two new letters, only to discover that the response, when tested, was not encouraging. On the advice of the support teacher, she decided to work on one letter at a time and to keep to her teaching methods. This achieved a better rate of progress over the next few weeks, but Callum had problems when the newly learnt letters were combined. A change in the teaching approach was decided upon in the hope of achieving greater success.

Callum was introduced to a Sound Lotto game which he played with other pupils. His teacher decided to revisit some of his newly learnt letters using materials from 'Letterland'. (This is a teaching approach that assigns pictorial characters to each letter. It is backed up by a wealth of support material.)

Finally, she introduced letters into an area of the curriculum in which Callum did well: art. He painted his new letters, created designs based on their shape and the Letterland characters and listened to songs linked to letter sounds. His progress was more marked and by the end of a six-week programme, he had reliably learnt nine new letter sounds which he could recognize in words and in spelling tasks.

What had been learnt throughout this process?

- Callum *can learn*, but he learns slowly.
- He copes better with *smaller steps* than those that other children in his class can manage.
- He needs a fair degree of *revision and relearning for newly learnt material*.
- Callum *seems to* learn more successfully when the same task is approached in a variety of different ways.
- Art *might be a route to success* in other areas of the curriculum.
- Callum *likes to achieve success*, but he prefers a quiet, private celebration, rather than a big class show.
- Callum *can generalize to other areas*, e.g. from reading to spelling, but he still needs a fair degree of prompting.

This illustrates a real situation in which slow but steady and reliable progress was sustained. By using the model on a variety of areas, his teacher discovered a lot about Callum and his responses to her teaching. His curricular needs differ from those of his peers, but through successes and failures it is now becoming apparent how best to teach him and how to adapt material for this purpose. In the process, his teacher is also acquiring new skills and a good dose of job satisfaction.

PROCEDURES AND PROCESSES

In this section we take a broader view of the classroom and those aspects of procedures which are within teachers' control. We will concentrate on selected topics: group work; involving children in decisions about their work; classroom organization; and the adaptation of written materials to enhance pupils' access to the curriculum. We are aware, all the time, of the need to modify or adapt aspects of the learning environment in ways which should enhance children's success while not isolating them either physically or with regard to the curriculum. Once again, there are no textbook solutions. We present ideas and approaches which we invite teachers to consider and to evaluate for their respective situations.

Group work

There is an entirely understandable temptation when planning work for pupils with learning problems to conceive of the child as needing to work at his own pace and, therefore, alone. This can result in the pupil's becoming isolated, maybe in connection with the materials used and sometimes even physically. In isolating the child, however, the teacher fails to make use of the powerful tool of co-operative or group work. In their useful book, Wade and Moore (1987) give practical advice over the management of small-group work with particular regard to the importance of language development. They list a baker's dozen of benefits from small-group work. The outcomes they describe include self-expression, less dependency on the teacher, experience of co-operative work, a sense of social identity and the development of commitment through the motivating power of such work. This may seem somewhat idealistic; group work may be construed more cynically as the brighter pupils doing the work and the others simply copying. Yet as long as the process is well managed and constructed, the reality may be somewhat different from this.

It is interesting to note that ways of working which have been used successfully in primary schools have started to be used in secondary schools. This has come about as a result of changes to examination structures and the greater importance assigned to course work. The same sort of stimulus was provided by the emphasis, in certain parts of the National Curriculum, on group work activities involving discovery learning and experimentation. Well-managed activities ensure that the purpose of the piece of work is not simply to find the *answer*, but to engage in debate, to exchange ideas and make use of practical skills. These are aspects where pupils can show their particular strengths and interests, and group work allows teachers to arrange activities to make best use of the particular interests and strengths of pupils.

When organizing a group it is necessary to limit its size to around six and to ensure a spread of ability. All members need to understand exactly what they are aiming to produce and how the task can be divided up. Key roles can be assigned and the children encouraged to report back to their team at intervals. The format for the eventual product can vary; it need not be a piece of written work. Oral presentation (using a tape-recorder), drawing, building a model are among the alternative options. To make sure that pupils really do understand a task, it is a good idea to ask them to explain it to the teacher or, under supervision, to another pupil. Before giving the green light for 'Go', the teacher must check that pupils with learning difficulties know exactly what is required, for unless they do, they may be additionally constrained.

In arranging group tasks, the teacher needs to take account of the existing attainments of pupils, their interests and what it is hoped the child will learn from the activities. It is also valuable to identify what experience of groups the pupils may have had with other teaching colleagues. When assessing the benefits of group activities, it is important to appreciate the degree of social and interpersonal skills involved. As we all know, working collaboratively in a group is not easy; it requires skills which develop only over time. For this reason alone, the introduction of group work should be gradual, to enable pupils, and indeed any teacher who is new to it, to come to terms with the organizational and skill requirements. Two constitutes a group and is a good starting point.

During the activity, the teacher should move from one group to the next, taking particular care to ensure that the pupils with learning problems are not being left out, are not being swamped by stronger characters and are not sticking on particular problems. A fair degree of social engineering, subtle cajoling and the judicious use of prompting, together with appropriate rewarding, can all be necessary. Feedback time at the end of the session is crucial, giving a purpose to the activity and allowing the teacher to assess what particular pupils have contributed and learnt. This session will also help the teacher to

49

plan appropriately for the next set of activities. This is another example of the assessment-through-teaching model in action, evaluated practice being the basis on which pupil progress and teaching strategies are analysed.

Involving children in decisions about their learning

If we consider our own learning problems and learning styles, most of us would probably admit to wanting to be involved in the planning of that learning and in the assessment of our progress. We would probably also like to know what we have to learn in the long term and why this is necessary. Children react in the same way, so to explain to a child why he or she is being encouraged to learn a particular skill or take part in an activity can result in stronger, more positive and purposeful attitudes to learning. The level of explanation clearly has to vary with the child, but even the simple 'If you learn this, you will be able to do . . .' has distinct advantages over requiring apparently (to the child) purposeless learning.

While a broad-based range of activities through which to cover the curriculum is being planned, decisions will need to be made about what can be attempted next. On this, even the youngest pupil may have an opinion and, wherever possible, pupils' views should guide the planning. (This kind of involvement also helps ensure that pupils understand the purpose and nature of the activities.) Providing feedback on progress is a way to keep a child wanting to learn; acknowledging success should encourage him to keep going, as long as he is making progress. All these tactics can be helpful in ensuring a child's progress in learning, which is often a more difficult task than identifying the learning problem.

A further way in which to encourage progress, while at the same time involving the child, is to use a form of record-keeping which the child understands. This could be in the form of a simple chart, preferably one which the child can complete (e.g. colouring steps on a ladder). With older pupils one obviously uses more sophisticated explanations and record-keeping systems. The principle remains, however, of involving the pupils in the planning and charting of their own learning and progress. These records can form the basis of talks (it would be unrealistic to refer to them as discussions) about their overall progress and areas for future work. Such records can also be used to provide parents with information about their child's progress, and help them become more involved.

Classroom organization

Primary school teachers very largely control the whole show inside their classrooms, although collaborative teaching methods (previously the domain of the secondary teachers) are increasingly being used by primary teachers seeking to pool expertise and share particular strengths. Nevertheless, the overall organization of the classroom is in the hands of one teacher. There are a number of key factors to consider in this connection, particularly when trying to provide for the pupil with learning difficulties.

The ordering of the day is important. Different teaching activities suit different times. Prime learning time is not just before lunch, nor at the end of the day: these times may be ideal for an oral activity or the traditional story, always with the emphasis (especially for children with learning difficulties) on checking comprehension and providing opportunities for discussions. The start of a session is usually the most productive time to devote to slow learners, once the larger group has been settled into their work.

The day needs to be balanced, not only with regard to the subjects covered, but also taking into account the range of activities presented to the pupil. Direct teaching should not be concentrated into one long block of time, but should be introduced sparingly but powerfully. The old teaching adage of 'a little and often' has much to commend it, in our view. Equally, direct teaching does not have to take place only on a one-to-one basis. Small, well-run groups provide the participants with a lot of teacher instruction, the chance to learn from other pupils and to make mistakes in a relatively protected environment, and a situation in which social skills may be learnt.

Managing a classroom is really a skilled art, requiring the teacher to keep a lot of children, all with different needs, ticking over. Children with learning problems will require attention on a more regular basis than their peers. These children therefore need to be positioned near to, but not directly under the nose of, the teacher. To place them so close would be to give the children, and their classmates, a very clear and possibly unhelpful message as to how their particular difficulties are perceived. It is one thing to do this with a pupil whose behaviour is unacceptable and quite another for the child with learning problems.

Pacing is an important part of organizing the school day. Teachers and children, especially children who are struggling, become tired. Athletes need to have recovery times built into their regular training programmes; the children we have been describing equally need recovery time, consisting of easier activities and an interesting degree of variation.

If all of this section seems like good common-sense teaching practice, remember that this is indeed the case. The requirement is, however, to take extra care over those factors, recognizing their vital significance in the designing of a supportive and productive learning environment.

Even an empty classroom can say a great deal about the attitudes of its key player, the teacher. How work is celebrated and presented should reflect relative rather than absolute achievements; pieces of less than perfect work on the wall can mean an enormous amount to the child who has struggled to achieve such a level. Books and other learning resources left out should again reflect the varying levels and needs of the class group. Hiding the 'lower'-level reading books away, particularly on parents' day, conveys a hurtful message to the pupils who use such texts. In short, the classroom layout should be designed to ensure that *all* pupils feel a sense of ownership in that space, rather than feeling it to be the exclusive province of the high achievers.

Adapting written materials

The development of the DART (Directed Activities Related to Text) techniques has taken place, largely in the secondary sector, in response to demands for existing materials to be adapted to give pupils with learning problems better access to them. In addition, the requirement was to enhance the child's skills at gleaning information from written texts using innovative and yet essentially simple ideas. The main reference work in this area is *The Effective Use of Reading* (Lunzer and Gardner, 1984); the main tools are careful preparation, creativity, versatility, sharing ideas among teachers, evaluation in the light of pupil responses and hard work. The techniques can be used well in group work to stimulate conversation about the piece and the set task. In essence, the approach helps pupils to get to the meaning of written material.

Examples culled from our own experience would include:

- Cutting up a text and asking the pupil to place the components in the correct order.
- Asking the pupil to highlight phrases which provide answers to comprehension questions.
- Separating pictures from texts and asking pupils to rejoin the two.
- Providing clues or cues within the text, either by marking or highlighting, as to the answers to particular questions.
- Using the cloze technique, removing words or phrases from the text and asking pupils to replace them.
- Inviting pupils to predict the range of outcomes possible from a particular passage, when the last section has been removed.

- Presenting a text in which two stories have been entangled and asking the pupil to separate them out.

Inviting and encouraging the child to *pull out* the meaning behind the words in these ways, even if it sometimes involves the teacher in extra preparation, is well worth while.

As a rule, teachers faced with the demands of pupils with varying learning difficulties need to break away vehemently from the constraints of materials and packages geared to the mythical 'average' child. The needs of children with learning difficulties are unlikely to be accommodated by the use of texts, source materials, reference works and activity sheets which are pitched at a higher than appropriate level.

Once again, the teacher needs to search out more suitable materials by asking her colleagues, support staff and special school colleagues. One of the DART techniques that can be put to good use is to adapt all forms of material by chopping up existing pieces and supplementing or modifying them where necessary. Teachers should also experiment in producing their own materials, based on the knowledge of a pupil's capabilities and with regard to the intended teaching outcomes. There is no creed about the sort of materials which children experiencing learning difficulties require; it is really a question of finding out what works with particular children and having the confidence to experiment and to be creative.

When selecting and compiling any form of teaching or pupil work materials, it is important to bear in mind the particular interests of the children concerned, their attainments to date and their self-respect. It is demeaning for older children to be asked to work on books which they know are in regular use by pupils much younger than themselves; probably more mortifying is the fact that their classmates will know it. Equally, the subject matter or storyline has to be at an age-appropriate rather than an attainment-appropriate level. Gender-based and cultural aspects should also be considered when selecting materials. For those practitioners who are interested in a more refined level of material adaptation, linked to a detailed curriculum analysis and the use of behavioural objectives, there is a useful section in Solity and Bull (1987, pp. 61–8).

Parental involvement

Much has been written about parental involvement and of the general gains that have been achieved. The most successful initiatives have been built around detailed projects which have been aimed at involving parents in a regular and organized way in supporting the work of the school. Such endeavours are not to be recommended for the teacher who is relatively new to the profession. Almost inevitably, certain parents will ask how they can work with their child at home to assist the teacher. Such offers should be utilized as valuable resources, but they will need to be managed to avoid the well-meaning parent actually doing more damage than good. Key points to be considered are:

- Limit the amount of time allocated in the home for work that is obviously school work, particularly during the school week. Children are often physically and emotionally tired at the end of the school day, as are parents. Any direct teaching should preferably be in the form of a game.
- Parents will tend to teach how *they* were taught, which may not necessarily be in line with current methods. The last thing we need is to confuse pupils who are experiencing learning difficulties. A little time spent explaining how suitable words are approached phonically or how decomposition in subtractions is tackled can save difficult problems. Teachers may need to explain their objectives or teaching goals to such parents and show them how they can help.
- Parents should be encouraged to spend time reading to and with their children, not only to reinforce teaching methods, but especially to share in the fun that books can bring to a child. Such sessions can serve as good role models for pupils who may be fearful of the printed word.
- The power of play should never be understated. So much can be taught incidentally and through imitation. This can have a beneficial effect on all cognitive, language, motor, social and literacy skills.
- It is essential to maintain regular contact between parents and the teacher either by short meetings or written reports in both directions. *Regular* communication seems to be the hallmark of success in home–school relationships.

Parents and volunteers can provide valuable support in the classroom, helping pupils practise skills that need to be reinforced, but obviously such additional input needs to be managed by the teacher and used in moderation if the classroom is not to become swamped.

CHAPTER SUMMARY

There is no single way to meet the needs of pupils who are described as exhibiting learning difficulties.

The curriculum and its modifications are key tools for teachers. The message of this chapter has been that teachers need to experiment with a variety of curriculum-related topics, and choose methods that suit their situation. Objectives still have much to offer teachers and pupils but in a form which is considerably more flexible than was advocated in the past.

We described the principles of assessment through teaching in some detail because this approach offers practitioners a way of evaluating the efficacy of their teaching.

Teacher and pupil attitudes are of crucial importance, a belief that informs our presentation of a range of practical strategies. Classroom organization in its broadest sense, including the adaptation of materials, is under teachers' control and can be put to good use in attempting to meet pupils' needs. The main section of the chapter provided an overview of factors that teachers could consider in formulating their response to the needs of pupils. Parents can be useful allies; key pointers to maximize and to influence this resource were outlined.

The chapter is essentially optimistic, recognizing and supporting the view that the majority of pupils who experience learning problems can and should be taught alongside their peers. To attempt to do so is not an easy undertaking; reassuringly, the rewards of even partial success can be significant.

SUGGESTIONS FOR FURTHER READING

Bennet, N., Desforges, C., Cockburn, A. and Wilkinson, B. (1984) *The Quality of Pupil Learning Experiences*. London: Lawrence Erlbaum. A detailed academic approach to the problems experienced by teachers in task- and activity-setting. The book draws upon the researchers' detailed observations of primary teachers, and its practical recommendations make valuable starting points.

Lunzer, E., Gardner, K., Davies, F. and Green, T. (1984) *Learning from the Written Word*. Edinburgh: Oliver & Boyd. A wide-ranging, practical source book for ideas related to the DART approach. The emphasis is upon improving pupils' access to written material. An extremely useful and stimulating resource.

Norwich, B. (1990) *Reappraising Special Needs Education*. London: Cassell. A balanced overview of special needs education which includes excellent chapters on curriculum design, with particular reference to using behavioural objectives, and to the 1981 Education Act.

Pratt, D. (1980) *Curriculum Design and Development*. New York: Harcourt Brace Jovanovich. This is really advanced-level curriculum planning using behavioural objectives in a variety of forms. There are also detailed accounts of the arguments concerning the use of objectives.

National Curriculum Council (1989) *Two: A Curriculum for All:*

Special Educational Needs in the National Curriculum. York: NCC. This is essential reading for teachers in that it represents an attempt to translate rhetoric into practical examples. To some extent it succeeds, at least in providing detailed examples in the Foundation subjects.

Solity, J.E. and Bull, S. (1987) *Special Needs: Bridging the Curriculum Gap*. Milton Keynes: Open University Press. In the context of this chapter, the book is a valuable source of examples of the Task Analysis approach, the use of objectives, assessment through teaching and the evaluation of published materials.

Topping, K. (1988) *The Peer Tutoring Handbook: Promoting Co-operative Learning*. London: Croom Helm. A detailed account of how to establish such a scheme. It includes many useful tips for working collaboratively with parents.

Wade, B. and Moore, M. (1987) *Special Children . . . Special Needs*. London: Robert Royce. This is an easy book to read, thanks to the authors' relaxed style and their use of anecdotal descriptions of particular children. They emphasize practical considerations and include a list of useful contact addresses for organizations concerned with special needs children.

CHAPTER 5

Children with emotional and behavioural difficulties

CHAPTER OVERVIEW

We begin by exploring what it is that makes some children's behaviour problematic for teachers, and then consider ways of categorizing such children and why this is so difficult to do. The third section looks at approaches to working with difficult children and introduces a behavioural technique. We then look at some of the support that is available to teachers, both within schools and from outside agencies, and at the range of special provision, outside mainstream schools, for children with emotional and behavioural difficulties. The later part of the chapter is devoted to the role of teachers in relation to children who have suffered or who are suffering from abuse, and to children who may have transient special needs at some period during their school career.

WHAT MAKES CHILDREN'S BEHAVIOUR A PROBLEM?

In our discussion of the concept of learning difficulties it became apparent that their identification depended heavily on *context*. The definition of problem behaviour is likewise, and even more so, dependent on the context in which it occurs. Very often what seems a problem to one person does not seem a problem at all to someone else. Similarly, behaviour which is perfectly acceptable in one situation may result in a severe reprimand in another. There is a high degree of subjectivity involved in judgements about behaviour and, consequently, individuals' reactions and their attempts to change or manage behaviour also vary widely. A key factor in how teachers react to children's behaviour is the teacher's *attitudes*.

Attitudes

The attitudes which teachers bring into the classroom, along with their beliefs and values, will to a large extent determine what they are prepared to tolerate and what they see as acceptable behaviour. Some need to feel 'in control' at all times and in order to achieve this adopt a very 'controlling' style of teaching; others may feel that the children can learn more effectively by sharing the responsibility for what takes place in the classroom. In this case some of the control will be shifted from the teacher to the children. The personality of the teacher and the way in which she construes her role are thus bound to affect her attitudes to behaviour. Her attitudes then determine, in part, the standards of behaviour she requires and her reactions to good and bad behaviour.

Context

In the same way that definitions of learning difficulties may shift from school to school, so behaviour problems can be construed differently, even between classes and between teachers in the same school. A child who has been a 'little demon' for a whole year in one class can be viewed as 'a delight' by his next class teacher. How much the child has changed and how much is due to teacher perceptions is open to speculation. Varying tolerance levels among teachers can cause problems within a school if it means that school and class rules come into conflict. Such a situation can cause major problems for the pupils, who have to learn very quickly what is permissible and what is not, for each teacher with whom they have contact.

We shall be discussing the benefits of clearly defined and complementary systems of rules in the next chapter. However, it is worth stating at this point that very often teachers may have to sacrifice some of their long-held views and practices because they do not tally with those of the school in which they have found employment. A somewhat *laissez-faire* teacher might need to impose a stricter system of discipline because the ethos of the school demands it; conversely, a more traditional teacher could find herself 'at sea' when a new headteacher introduces more liberal ideas into a school. The process of accommodating and adapting to such changes can be very difficult. For some teachers the gap between their style and the school's is too wide and they may decide to change school, or have it decided for them. Either way, for a school to run well and smoothly, the attitudes and beliefs of the staff should be in harmony.

Emotional responses

Unlike learning difficulties, behavioural difficulties in children often provoke an emotional response on the part of the teacher. A sense of anger, frustration, sadness and often fear is engendered by a child exhibiting extreme or uncontrolled behaviour. These emotions, if not anticipated, can be overwhelming and leave the teacher feeling helpless and out of control. It is therefore useful for teachers, before coming into contact with difficult children, to have considered the range of behaviour which they might encounter. They can then prepare suitable coping strategies and will probably find they are not 'thrown' by their own feelings.

Very often, as Wade and Moore (1987) point out, in cases where a particular programme of behaviour management is being implemented with a child, some immediate positive change in the child's behaviour will result. However, this change may be followed by a reversal and a deterioration, which can be very disheartening for the teacher. If this is anticipated, however, then the teacher can be prepared and may well be able to use strategies designed to maintain the momentum of the programme. She might also feel less downhearted at the apparent short-term failure.

Links between behaviour and learning

It is difficult to discuss learning and behaviour separately: they are totally interlinked, and in any teaching situation the effects of learning on behaviour and behaviour on learning cannot be ignored. We do not have enough space here to analyse these effects in any detail, but will mention two key concepts: *motivation* and *self-esteem*. For the sake of brevity, suffice it to say that, if a child is well motivated, perhaps by a well-structured and interesting curriculum, his behaviour is likely to be better. Looking at it from another perspective, if children are motivated to conform to class rules, for example by means of a reward system, then their learning is likely to improve.

Self-esteem is difficult to measure, but a child with low self-esteem is likely to perform badly both in terms of the work he produces and the behaviours he exhibits. Therefore, techniques for increasing self-esteem, both in a group setting and for individuals, can lead to improvements in behaviour and learning.

Terminology

The categories used in special education have changed dramatically over the years. For most people working in the field, these changes are seen as long overdue. Attempts have been made to define more accurately what difficulties certain groups of children present, rather than attempting to assign a general label to them. The term 'maladjustment' has been widely used since 1945 to describe a broad grouping of children. However, the Warnock Committee, when considering categories of handicap, felt that 'maladjustment' was not a helpful term and so introduced the term 'children with emotional and behavioural difficulties' (EBD). Their phrase is still, many would argue, unclear and subjective. Wolfendale (1987, p. 61) gives some insight into why this might be so: 'Terminology . . . is confused and confusing since it mirrors the never-to-be-resolved debates about aetiology and cause and effect.'

The reasons why children exhibit behavioural and emotional difficulties remain especially equivocal. The vast amount of literature on the subject reflects the various attempts to describe, explain and categorize such children and their behaviour. The ideas of some authors have proved more useful and long-lasting than others. The Underwood Report (1955) attempted to describe maladjustment in children by reference to a list of behaviours which either alone or in groups might be said to be maladjusted. Later, Rutter (1975) provided a set of nine criteria which can be used as a way of estimating the level of a possible abnormality in a child's behaviour. These criteria include:

- the age and sex appropriateness of the behaviour;
- its persistence;
- the life circumstances;
- the socio-cultural setting;
- the extent of the disturbance;
- the type of symptom;
- the severity and frequency of symptoms;
- changes in behaviour;
- situation specificity.

Laslett, in *Educating Maladjusted Children* (1977), attempted to provide a text which synthesized theory and practical advice on the management of maladjusted children. Whatever the terms used, the reasons behind maladjustment, disturbance or emotional and behavioural difficulties are undoubtedly many, complex and interlinked.

Explaining difficult behaviour

The variety of labels, categorizations, conditions and their aetiologies is a vast minefield. It would be inappropriate in a text such as this to offer any new or definitive explanation. Instead, we will comment briefly from our own experience and refer to a text which we have found useful in trying to identify the reasons behind difficult behaviour.

By far the most significant factor influencing behaviour must be home and family. In our work as educational psychologists we see children in nurseries, even sometimes in playgroups, whose behaviour already gives cause for concern. Lack of parenting skills accounts for many of children's later problems; the learning patterns established at home during the pre-school days can cause major problems when children enter formal education. Obviously, for many youngsters who are exhibiting early signs of difficult behaviour, help is available before they are of school age. We shall be looking at sources and types of help in Chapter 8.

A book we have found helpful in this area is Montgomery's *Managing Behaviour Problems* (1989), which considers in some depth social and cognitive factors that may give rise to 'behaviour disturbances', and offers the following possible reasons for what Montgomery terms 'unsocialized behaviour problems':

- rejection by parents;
- neglect by parents;
- immature parents;
- indulgent or compensating parents.

She offers brief explanations as to why these particular parenting characteristics might result in certain types of behaviour difficulty. Some of her explanations seem rather speculative, but many examples ring true and new teachers especially may find some of her ideas useful.

Inevitably, most of the factors discussed are beyond the influence of the school and teacher, and for this reason do not warrant lengthy discussion here. We shall focus on factors which are within the teacher's control and influence, such as behaviour within the classroom and interactions with others.

Another approach to categorizing problem behaviour was taken by the committee chaired by Lord Elton that investigated discipline in schools. Behavioural descriptors were used as a way of collecting information from teachers about the children in their classes. The committee did not attempt to delve into possible causes of disruption, but instead highlighted the evidence of good practice that was found.

The Elton Report

In 1989 a report entitled *Discipline in Schools: Report of the Committee of Inquiry* was published and has come to be known as the Elton Report after Lord Elton, who chaired the committee. The brief of the inquiry was to consider what

> action could be taken by the government, LEAs, governors, headteachers, teachers and parents to
>
> secure the orderly atmosphere necessary in schools for effective teaching and learning to take place.
>
> This aim demonstrates admirably the link between behaviour and learning. It highlights the fact that effective discipline and good behaviour management are essential prerequisites to effective teaching and learning.

The Elton Report was compiled from extensive evidence made up of individual submissions, interviews and questionnaires mainly provided by teachers. Its findings and its 138 recommendations for action make interesting reading. With reference to the types of difficult behaviour identified by teachers, there was overwhelming evidence that the vast majority of teachers have to deal with minor disruptions on a regular basis. It is these types of persistent irritating behaviours, such as 'being out of their seats', 'talking out of turn' and 'distracting others in the class', which proved the most wearing and frustrating for teachers. This finding was in stark contrast to the steady stream of press reports which gave an impression of violence and aggression being on the increase in schools. The evidence suggested that this was not the case, with only a few teachers reporting incidents involving physical aggression. Obviously, well-run, orderly schools are not newsworthy, nor will they ever be.

APPROACHES TO WORKING WITH CHILDREN WITH EMOTIONAL AND BEHAVIOURAL DIFFICULTIES

Over the past half century, since it has been acknowledged that some children do suffer from emotional problems and do present management difficulties for their carers, a variety of approaches have been tried in order to help such children. Some approaches have aimed to 'cure' the children and some have been more concerned with the management and containment of their behaviour. At the present time, a range of approaches are used, some by specialists and some by practising teachers.

Children with problems deemed to be severe, even perhaps bordering on the psychiatric, may require some form of *psychotherapy* provided by a child psychiatrist, a specialist social worker or a child psychotherapist. This may include individual work or group work, or may centre around work with the child and his family. The therapy usually takes place over a long period.

Counselling is a more familiar vehicle for working with children on an individual basis, although it more often occurs and is more effective with adolescents. For any counselling to be effective it should not take place in a vacuum, but must be part of an approach which also includes examining the context and identifying the roles of those involved.

At one time many secondary schools employed their own school counsellor who was able to support many pupils on an individual basis. For a number of reasons these posts are now few and far between as the pastoral and disciplinary systems in many schools have been subsumed under one role. Counselling is still available for some children and is sometimes undertaken by members of support services who visit schools.

Another widely used approach to preventing and ameliorating behavioural problems is to tackle some of the issues directly through teaching. This can be approached directly through the curriculum, often under headings such as 'personal, social and moral education' or by a topic approach which engages children in discussion about ways of behaving and the rights and wrongs of situations. Skilful teachers can adapt some of the available published materials to include issues that may be of local concern, such as, for example, bullying, or an incident involving racist language. Many practitioners feel that such approaches gain by being part of the curriculum.

Allied to this are assessment-through-teaching approaches which operate similarly to those described on pp. 42–8. Solity and Raybould (1988) define five steps which can be used in order to improve a child's social behaviour:

- Decide which personal and social skills are expected.
- Determine what personal and social skills the child has learnt.
- Decide which personal and social skills to teach.
- Decide how to teach.
- Assess the pupil's progress.

This approach means that, in effect, the teacher must construct a 'behavioural curriculum' for the class. Such a curriculum would serve a dual purpose. Primarily it would provide a framework into which all class rules and procedures could be fitted. It would also mean that any programmes designed to improve an individual pupil's behaviour could include targets from within the whole-class curriculum. There are a number of similar approaches which use direct teaching to improve behaviour. Procedures from social skills training have been used effectively with primary school children (see Spence and Shepherd, 1983).

Many of these interventions have elements in common and can be termed 'behavioural approaches'. We shall look more closely at this area, as it has much to offer teachers and also forms the basis of most packages and materials being used in schools.

A behavioural approach

An essentially pragmatic approach, it seeks to provide clear plans of action that result in observable changes in behaviour. The assumptions basic to most commonly used behavioural approaches are made explicit in Cheeseman and Watts's manual for teachers (1985) and can be summarized roughly as follows (Wolfendale, 1987):

- behaviour is learnt;
- if it has not been learnt it can be taught;
- most child behaviour problems are simply excesses or deficits of behaviour common to all children;
- learning must be within a social context;
- the teacher is the most appropriate change agent within schools.

Many authors have based their advice to teachers on very similar assumptions, and our experience has convinced us that they provide a useful springboard for introducing practical classroom strategies (see pp. 82–7). One of the main differences between behavioural approaches and other, earlier approaches is that behavioural approaches focus on observable behaviours in the here and now and on what can be done to change existing behaviour patterns. Earlier approaches paid more attention to underlying causes of behaviour, and intervention strategies tended to be more long-term. Often their direct effects on behaviour were less obvious and, in many cases, they failed to provide any immediate and practical strategies to tackle the behaviour.

Throughout this book we have stressed that special needs children do not, in the main, require 'special' teaching or treatment. In the same way, the strategies that can be employed to 'improve' children's behaviours can also be used to improve overall classroom management.

USING OTHERS TO HELP TEACHERS

Before considering what an individual teacher on her own can do to manage the behaviour of difficult pupils in her class, we shall look at some of the sources of support that might be available to classroom teachers.

Support within the school

A new teacher will find that one of the best ways of gaining immediate support, and possibly practical ideas, is to talk in the staffroom about how to cope with any 'difficult' children in her class. Doing so used to be taken as a sign of weakness or incompetence, but most staff members are now more understanding and supportive, possibly because it is generally accepted that *all* teachers experience problems at one time or another. It helps to talk in terms of what you are trying to do and are thinking of trying next. A positive approach elicits sympathy; moaning does not.

Some schools have more formal mechanisms set up for helping teachers to deal with difficult children. Since the publication of the Elton Report in 1989, there have been various government funding initiatives in this sector. Education Support Grants and similar funds have allowed local authorities to improve their support to schools. In some cases, this has meant establishing or increasing their Behaviour Support Services or equivalents. In other cases, schools have been helped to set up their own 'in-house' mechanisms for supporting teachers. Some have chosen to appoint 'behaviour co-ordinators' within the school and others have set up formalized support groups, which meet regularly to discuss a variety of issues and problems.

Outside support agencies

There are a range of support agencies for teachers in most local authorities. They vary in their approach, particularly in the extent to which they will deal with individual children outside the classroom or work through the class teacher. Increasingly, support staff are encouraging class teachers to use them as consultants, there to provide ideas, resources, support and sometimes just a sympathetic and encouraging ear. This is particularly the case for educational psychologists, who were specifically recommended for a consultancy role in the Elton Report (recommendation 124). The Report also suggested that psychologists should be used to provide advice to headteachers on management issues, and should be invited into schools to act as consultants over whole-school behaviour management. For an example of this approach, see Leadbetter *et al.* in *Psychological Services for Primary Schools* (Lindsay and Miller, 1991).

Other agencies, such as Education Social Work Services, can provide useful home contact for children with behaviour difficulties which occur across settings. Some Psychological Services and Child Guidance Services have specialist social workers who are able to work alongside psychologists to help with children whose difficulties are severe. There are also behaviour support teachers in some authorities who can be called upon to help in a variety of ways with children's behaviour problems. They may, in some cases, provide individual support for a child within the class on a regular basis. They may help organize and set up a behaviour programme for the youngster. In some cases, they may be linked to external support bases, such as guidance centres, and so able to withdraw the child, if necessary. They will also be able to plan integration and reintegration programmes for children.

The role demarcations between these various agencies are becoming blurred. In this area, as in the area of child abuse and child protection, all professionals are being urged to work together co-operatively to ensure that children receive the best support available. In this way the school, the home and the support agencies are more likely to provide a co-ordinated response to a child who is in need of help.

PROVISION FOR CHILDREN WITH EMOTIONAL AND BEHAVIOURAL DIFFICULTIES

For children whose problems are particularly complex, severe and/or long-standing, the option of staying in mainstream schooling is not viable. Local authorities apply differing policies and use a range of provision to cater for such children (cf. the discussion in Chapter 2 on the integration of special needs pupils).

An approach previously much used was to group pupils who were presenting disruptive and difficult behaviour in one place, either attached to a mainstream school or in a different location altogether. This so-called 'sin-bin' unfortunately tended to ensure that the behaviour of many of the children deteriorated; and often children who entered such a unit for short-term placements became so influenced by their peers that reintegration into their original school became impossible. Such *'on-'* and *'off-site'* provision still exists in various forms across the United Kingdom. In some authorities, a child needs to be issued with a Statement of Special Educational Needs under section 7 of the Education Act 1981 before he can be admitted to this form of special provision, even on a short-term or part-time basis; in other areas, he can gain admission after the various relevant professionals have discussed and agreed on this line.

Most local authorities use, to a greater or lesser degree, *special schools* which cater for children with behavioural and emotional difficulties. These schools usually have high pupil–teacher ratios and employ teachers who have some specialized training in dealing with 'disturbed' children. The techniques they employ include those detailed earlier in this chapter but, because of the smaller number of pupils, they are able to undertake more individualized programmes with children and engage in more counselling.

Very often, children who are suffering from emotional disturbance or are exhibiting severe behavioural problems are referred to *residential schools*. This can be for a 5-day-a-week placement, the child returning home at weekends, or for 52 weeks a year, or any combination in between. The reason for referral is usually that home circumstances are not helping with the child's overall development at that time. For some children, a year away at a crucial or particularly difficult time can prove to be very helpful; for others it becomes necessary for them to spend most of their school age years away from home. Some residential schools are known as *therapeutic communities* as they endeavour to provide more intensive therapy and support for the child as a main feature. Very few children are in need of this level or type of support.

When children are removed from their families, homes and neighbourhoods, the fundamental question to ask at all times, but in particular at reviews, is when and how the child can be returned to his home and his local school. If a child reaches school leaving age and is not familiar with his local community, it makes his settling into a new phase of life extremely difficult. Therefore, the ideal course is for the majority of children to rejoin their local school as soon as a placement is judged to be viable.

THE ABUSED CHILD

Over the past years it has seemed that the levels of child abuse, both physical and sexual, have increased. This perception is undoubtedly due, in part, to the increase in media interest in the subject and also to a general heightening of awareness on the part of families, professionals and society as a whole. Whether or not there has been a general increase, there is certainly a role for teachers both in preventing and in identifying abuse. There are now a number of published materials which schools can use to educate children about abuse in its various forms (Elliott and Marlin, 1986). Some schools have chosen to include the topic under Health Education and to ensure that all children have received some guidance by the time they leave primary school. Materials vary in the approach they take. Story books are available and can be read to the class as a whole or read by individuals as they choose. These may illustrate to children the dangers of talking to strangers or they may give examples of problems which have occurred in the home, involving members of the family or visitors to the home. The intention is to alert children to possible dangers but also to provide an opening for any child who may be suffering from abuse to talk to an appropriate adult about his problems.

Another approach is to use stimulus material, such as a video or visiting speaker (in some areas this means staff from the School Medical Service), to open up discussions with the children. The focus may be on teaching children to say 'No' if something is happening to them which makes them feel uncomfortable, or on alerting them to the difference between 'nice cuddles' and 'nasty cuddles'. The intention is to make pupils aware of their feelings and teach them that it is in order for them to object if they are unhappy with something that is happening to them and to tell someone about it.

The teacher's role

As well as actively raising children's awareness of abuse the teacher can play a very important part in its detection. It has been estimated that as many as 1 in 10 children suffer some form of abuse at some time in their lives, so it is likely that one or two children in every class have been affected. Abuse is not restricted to any one class of family or type of child; it occurs across the whole social spectrum.

Very often, the class teacher is the first person to notice that there is something wrong in a child's life, perhaps by observing marked changes in his behaviour. The child might single the teacher out on a number of occasions and try to talk about tangential subjects. Children's 'cries for help' often occur in their writing and drawing: maybe in a factual account of 'what happened at home at the weekend', or in an imaginative story, in which they display ideas or knowledge disturbing and undesirable in a child of that age.

Whatever the sign, the teacher's initial response is of great importance, for it may make the difference between the child being able to open up and so gain access to some help, or feeling rebuffed and unsuccessful and deciding to keep his troubles to himself. If you, the teacher, are approached it is best to listen to the child in the first instance, but then seek help as soon as possible from within the school to decide whether further steps should be taken. Teachers have a duty to inform the headteacher should there be any grounds to suspect that a child has been abused in any way. In most local authorities there are now set guidelines and procedures in place which detail what headteachers should do in such circumstances. Most guidelines require immediate contact with the local Social Services Department so that the department can judge whether or not further enquiries should be made.

Signs of abuse

It is difficult to give a definitive checklist for signs of abuse. Different authors have highlighted a variety of warning signs and symptoms, but none provides a 'hard and fast' list. An authority may have its own list, which it expects its teachers to use. Every teacher would be well advised to check whether such a document exists in her school.

Physical abuse is usually more easily detected than sexual abuse, often when children are changing for or taking part in PE lessons. Vigilant teachers may observe unusual markings or bruisings on a child's body, or they may notice a child constantly making excuses for not changing or not doing PE. This could, of course, be due to laziness or a dislike of the cold, but it may be due to much more serious reasons and need further consideration.

It is much harder to list significant behaviours which indicate that a child is suffering, or has suffered, from sexual abuse. Withdrawn behaviour, lack of concentration, excessive playing with their genitalia and hyperactivity have all been associated with abused children, as have overfamiliarity with one sex, or with one particular person, and a detachment from reality. It can be seen that this list contains some 'fuzzy' terms; and many of those behaviours could well be observed in children who are not being abused.

Any child who has been abused and is perhaps receiving treatment for this, possibly involving rehabilitation back into his family, will need sensitive treatment and support in school. It is possible that the child might have volatile outbursts and be quite unpredictable. The role of the class teacher and the school is to provide as stable, consistent and caring an environment as possible, so that the child can be sure of feeling safe in at least one part of his life.

TRANSIENT SPECIAL NEEDS

Although most of the children to whom we will be referring in this book have special needs which are in some way permanent and long-term, there are certain times in a child's life when he might have special educational needs for a short period. We are not referring here to children who are perhaps temporarily disabled by an accident or recovering from an illness, but rather those whose emotional well-being and therefore possibly their behaviour are temporarily affected.

The strategies we suggest in the following chapter, for tackling difficult behaviour and preventing disruption in the classroom, are appropriate for all children, whether their special needs are long- or short-term. However, if teachers are aware of children's particular problems then they can be more sensitive in their handling of them and more prepared for the changes in behaviour that may result.

Possible causes of short-term special needs

A common cause of upset in children's lives is changes in home circumstances, for instance a loss of some kind, be it a bereavement or the effective loss of a parent due to marital break-up. There may be a period of parental disharmony leading up to any separation and this is highly likely to affect children.

Another change that can affect children greatly is the addition of another child to the family. This might be a new baby, a child belonging to a new partner coming into the home, or a fostered or adopted child. A high proportion of children now live within a family which contains a step-parent and step-children or half-brothers and sisters. This can cause particular difficulties and can affect individual members of the family differentially.

Temporary problems may be caused for a child by changes at school. The change from infant to junior can be stressful in terms of the new work, the routines and expectations. Another school-related problem is change in social grouping; not the forming and re-forming of friendship groups that is a normal part of school life, but, for instance, the case in which a vulnerable child's best friend leaves the school and the child finds that he is the victim of bullying. If a teacher makes a point of watching the children, both in the class and also during their free time, then she may be more aware of the dynamics of the situation and be able to intervene at an early stage, thus preventing problems for the child concerned.

Short-term and transient special needs such as these can be viewed as difficult stages through which any child might pass, but his progress, emotional and educational, can be greatly eased by a sensitive and skilled teacher.

CHAPTER SUMMARY

We have indicated the central importance of attitude and context in individual teachers' definitions of problematic behaviour. Behaviour and learning and their interaction are discussed, both in terms of the differing emotional responses they provoke in teachers and in terms of the positive and negative effects they have on each other. In the second section we mentioned the terminology that has historically been used to describe and categorize children exhibiting difficult behaviour and we commended the Elton Report for its enlightened approach to this topic.

We then described some approaches to working with children with emotional and behavioural difficulties and recommended that a broadly behavioural perspective can help with problem definition and with intervention. Suggestions were made in the following section which aimed to help teachers to find support for themselves and for the children in their class. This support can come from within the school or can be requested from outside support agencies. It was stressed that dealing with such children is difficult and teachers should not be afraid to ask for help.

We described the variety of provision which is available outside mainstream schools for children with emotional and behavioural difficulties and we stressed that, if children are moved to residential provision, their reintegration into their neighbourhood and their local school is more difficult. Child abuse appears to be more prevalent in recent times. Whether or not this is the case, we discussed the need for teachers to be vigilant, knowledgeable, sensitive and professional. We described some of the more common signs of abuse and the times when teachers should be particularly concerned. Finally, we considered the times in a child's life when he may experience transient special needs. We examined causes and considered how early teacher intervention can serve to alleviate some of the problems. This chapter should be read alongside the next chapter, which considers in detail how individuals can improve their own handling and teaching of children with emotional and behavioural difficulties.

SUGGESTIONS FOR FURTHER READING

Department of Education and Science (1989) *Discipline in Schools. Report of the Committee of Inquiry chaired by Lord Elton* (Elton Report). London: HMSO. A very readable and informative government report, full of useful and sensible recommendations.

Elliott, M. (1985) *Preventing Child Sexual Assault: A Practical Guide to Talking to Children*. London: Bedford Square Press. A useful source book which could form the basis of an in-school programme or be used for teachers to develop individual skills.

Leydon, G. (1991) Mind the steps! The primary school and children in second families. In G. Lindsay and A. Miller (eds), *Psychological Services for Primary Schools*. Harlow: Longman. This contains a review of the prevalence of parental separation and some of the effects this can have on children.

Lindsay, G. and Miller, A. (eds) (1991) *Psychological Services for Primary Schools*. Harlow: Longman. A selection of contributions from authors who work closely with teachers and schools. It contains unusual chapters, such as one focusing on helping the rejected child.

Montgomery, D. (1989) *Managing Behaviour Problems*. Sevenoaks: Hodder & Stoughton. A comprehensive text which seeks to provide practical ideas for intervening in children's behaviour as well as considering possible causes.

Rutter, M., Maughan, B., Mortimore, P. and Ouston, J. (1979) *Fifteen Thousand Hours*. London: Open Books. A survey of practice in schools, providing useful data that many subsequent studies have used as their focus.

Spence, S. (1980) *Social Skills Training with Children and Adolescents: A Counsellor's Manual*. Windsor: NFER-Nelson. A handbook containing useful ideas for practical training workshops and some original materials for assessment.

Thacker, J. (1982) *Steps to Success: An Interpersonal Problem-Solving Approach for Children*. Windsor: NFER-Nelson. A practical set of materials which can be used with individuals or groups of top primary-age children. Contains plenty of stimulus material for discussion.

CHAPTER 6

Classroom techniques for dealing with difficult behaviour

CHAPTER OVERVIEW

This chapter complements the previous chapter in that it provides practical help for teachers in terms of both their classroom management skills and their handling of individual children who present problems. It begins by describing a problem-solving approach which can be applied in a variety of situations and which helps teachers to clarify concerns, select goals and decide on action plans. A detailed example of the problem-solving approach applied to a whole-class situation is included along with some guidelines for judging the seriousness of problems. The second part of the chapter considers classroom management skills and covers topics such as rules, rewards, sanctions, classroom organization, resources and personal teaching skills. Finally, some suggestions are made in terms of action plans for dealing with difficult children within the class. These include home–school books, daily report systems, contracts and self-monitoring systems.

A PROBLEM-SOLVING APPROACH

Very often, when teachers are trying to deal with a particularly difficult child or a class which is rowdy, lively and uncooperative, the number of problems seems so vast and the problems often seem so intractable that it is difficult to know where to start. The sheer scope and complexity can deter even the most skilful and experienced teacher from trying anything in a planned way. In this situation, or preferably before the situation has been reached, it is useful to be equipped with a strategy that can help tackle the problems systematically and restore a sense of being in control.

The approach outlined below is applicable to problems in everyday life, be they small or large. It is only one version of a widely used technique, and there are no right or wrong versions. Some include extra steps, or sequence the steps slightly differently, but the overall stages are the same. Within the school setting, it can be used to tackle problems at an individual, class, group or whole-school level.

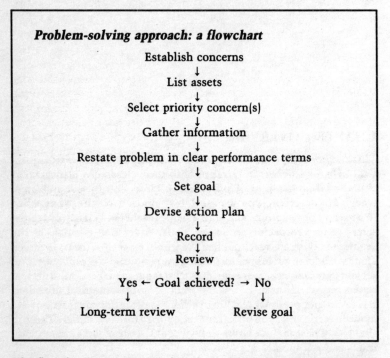

Problem-solving approach: a flowchart

Establish concerns
↓
List assets
↓
Select priority concern(s)
↓
Gather information
↓
Restate problem in clear performance terms
↓
Set goal
↓
Devise action plan
↓
Record
↓
Review
↓
Yes ← Goal achieved? → No
↓   ↓
Long-term review   Revise goal

The flowchart may suggest a lengthy and complex process but, once the technique has been used, it quickly becomes familiar and can form part of a general routine. Let us now examine each of the steps in turn and then consider an example.

Establish concerns

The first step is to list all the concerns about a given situation or child. At this stage they should simply be listed as problems, not as actions that need to be undertaken. Examples of concerns about PE lessons might be:

- noise levels too high;
- several accidents have occurred this term;
- some children regularly absenting themselves on PE day;
- I (teacher) feel particularly fraught at the end of the lesson.

Any concerns which are very similar should be grouped together. Also, any concerns which are *realistically* beyond the school's control should be eliminated or reformulated so that they can come within the school's influence. In other words, this procedure should not be seen as a 'miracle cure'; it can only help teachers to work effectively *within* their normal constraints.

List assets

Making a list of assets, an important step, involves focusing and noting down the *positives* about the situation or child. All too often when things are going wrong, it is easy to fall into the trap of thinking that nothing is right. Listing assets may help the teacher to view the situation in a more objective manner and may also provide angles which can be worked on to good effect at a later stage. Continuing our example of the PE lesson, teachers may note that:

- some of the low-achievers seem to enjoy the lessons and experience considerable success;
- new equipment is on order for next term after prompting from me (the teacher).

Select priority concern(s)

The selecting of priorities is probably one of the most important steps and one of the most difficult to accommodate. When things are going wrong, it is often tempting to try to tackle the problems from lots of different ways on the 'scatter' principle: that is, if you fire enough arrows at a target one of them will surely hit. We suggest that teachers do the opposite to this: thus once they have chosen a priority concern they can temporarily 'forget' all the others. In practice, we have found this selection to be most effective. Deciding on the priority concern is not as easy as it sounds. It might be worth asking the following questions:

How serious is the problem?
Is it a problem for other people?
How many children are involved?
How much time is taken up?
How often does the problem happen?

It is not always necessary to run through this process. Often the priority concern is clear from the beginning. However, it is still worth listing all concerns at the beginning, if only as a reminder of what else there is to work on, once this particular problem has been solved!

Another factor to consider when selecting a concern on which to work is to build on existing successes. So, if a similar problem has been successfully overcome by another teacher or if expert support is available to tackle one particular aspect of the problem, then the teacher may choose that concern over the others.

Gather information

The information gathered on the problem should be as objective and factual as possible. It may be possible to spend a week or so collecting some relevant data by observing the class carefully. Other sources of relevant information might include parents, the pupils themselves, or support agencies. This process serves a dual purpose. It may be that in the light of more objective data, the problem is seen to be more widespread than was first thought. Thus it may be necessary to involve more people or reconsider priorities. Or it may be that initial subjective impressions are not borne out by the information obtained by a more detailed look.

The second purpose of this information gathering is to provide some baseline data. Once an action plan has been implemented, it is then possible to collect the same information again and compare the results. It will then be clear how effective the intervention has been.

Restate problem in clear, performance terms

Having gathered some objective information, it should be possible to translate the concern (should this be necessary) into clear, performance terms. This means that no 'fuzzy' phraseology, no words which are clearly open to subjective interpretation should be used. For example, 'Aggressive outbursts from many of the boys spoil the lessons' might be rephrased as 'There are approximately two incidents involving physical contact between children during each lesson'. Everyone concerned is then clear about the nature of the problem. It is essential to have such unequivocal statements if later steps in the process are to be effective.

Set a goal

Goal setting is a daily activity for teachers and psychologists alike.

However, we may not be aware that we are doing this and may not be experienced in setting ourselves precise and prescriptive goals. Here is a definition of a goal; it is not the only one, nor necessarily the best, but it may help you understand why goals can be useful.

A goal

- is a statement of an intended outcome within an agreed area of concern;
- should be stated positively where possible;
- must include a time limit.

It can be valuable to practise writing goal statements for some routine areas of work. Particularly useful is the process of rewording some rather negative statements into positive ones, although this is not always possible. An example might be

To ensure all children have appropriate kit for PE

rather than

To stop children coming to their PE lessons with no kit

It is important to include a time limit so that the whole programme is not allowed to become open-ended and, as often happens, to peter out. A time limit is also necessary for the purposes of review.

Devise an action plan

This is arguably the most important part of the process as it relates directly to the planned intervention. Action plans can vary enormously: they might involve small changes to class routines or a particular programme involving individualized rewards for a particular child. Whatever the plan, it will need to be agreed by all parties concerned. Any plan of action should clearly state:

- the steps to be taken;
- who will be responsible for each step;
- details of records that will be kept to monitor or evaluate changes which are made;
- a date for review and an agreed method of review.

If all these factors are included, then it is much easier to decide on the next course of action at the review.

Record review

It is important that records are kept while the action plan is in progress. These records may be very simple – perhaps a star chart which is jointly completed by teacher and child. Alternatively, they may be

77

more complex, involving sets of observations or the collection of survey data. Whatever they include, it is vital that the records are accurately and continuously kept as they form the basis of decision making at the review. If others, such as parents or other school staff, are involved, the review may need to be a formal meeting. In other circumstances it can consist of a regular chat between the teacher and the child in question to discuss his progress and to plan the next stage.

Decisions taken at the review will depend on whether or not the goal has been achieved. As can be seen from the flowchart (p. 74), if the goal has been achieved, the teacher returns to the initial list and selects a different priority concern on which to work. However, if the goal has not been achieved, then goal or action plan may need revising slightly. Perhaps there was insufficient motivation for the child to change his behaviour or perhaps the time it would take to teach a group of children a new skill was under-estimated. Whatever the reason, guidance over where to go next can be gained by looking at the results over the time period, noting in particular when any changes were introduced into the programme.

This problem-solving approach may seem long-winded or laboured but it is necessary in the early stages to put in the time and effort to ensure sound problem assessment.

Example of the problem-solving approach

This example is taken from a junior school classroom where the following was seen by the teacher as being the broad problem area:

> Movement around the class and noise levels mean that work output is suffering.

Establish concerns

- A chair grates on the floor every time a child stands up.
- At any one time, several children are out of their seats.
- Levels of chat mean that I (the teacher) am constantly shouting over them.
- Certain children have complained that they cannot concentrate.
- Rearranging tables and chairs for group work takes too long.

List assets

- The room is large and quite bright.
- They responded quite well to the last class discussion about behaviour.

- I have been given a small sum of money to spend on equipment.
- There are a number of conscientious children in the class.

Select priority concern(s)

- At any one time several children are out of their seats.

Rationale: This would tackle the issues of both noise and movement. It would mean fewer distractions for the hard-working children and should ensure that all children have more actual working time if there were no reason for them to be out of their seats.

Gather information

I will use my classroom assistant's time to undertake some structured observation sessions to discover which children get out of their seats, why they are moving around and for how long.

Restate problem in clear performance terms

During a typical morning lesson (1 hour) there are, on average, 27 instances of children getting out of their seats.

Set goal

By the end of term (6 weeks), there will be no more than 10 instances of children getting out of their places during a typical one-hour lesson.

Devise action plan

- Use money that is immediately available to purchase extra basic equipment such as pens, crayons, rubbers and pencil sharpeners.
- Rearrange tables so that less movement of furniture is required for different activities.
- Discuss the problem with the class and aim to draw up a list of legitimate reasons for being out of your seat.
- Discuss with the head and at the next staff meeting the possibility of spending the extra capitation on carpeting the classrooms.

Record

For one lesson each week, my classroom assistant will record the number of 'out-of-seat' incidents (ideally, without the children knowing). We will plot the incidents on a graph on a weekly basis and share the results with the children.

Review

I will review the situation at the end of term and if necessary discuss further strategies with the children, the head and the classroom assistant.

Goal achieved!

The intervention proved very effective and out-of-seat behaviour was greatly reduced. The resulting graph is shown in Figure 6.1.

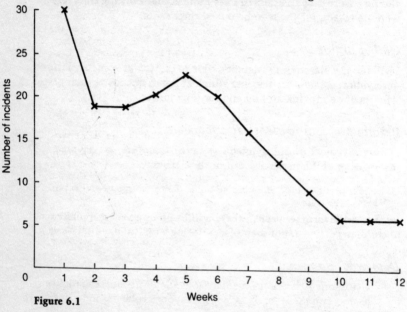

Figure 6.1

Having succeeded with her action plan, this teacher will choose something else to focus on, again something in which she can involve the class. The problem-solving approach can thus form part of a rolling programme which any teacher can undertake in order to ensure that her teaching is constantly developing and improving.

DECIDING ON THE SERIOUSNESS OF PROBLEMS

Many children's behavioural problems can quite usefully be viewed simply as excesses or deficits of normal behaviour for children of that age (Cheeseman and Watts, 1985). However, it is sometimes difficult to assess whether this is the case or whether a child is having particular problems and so is exhibiting extreme or unusual behaviours. A technique which may help the teacher to decide whether or not specific action should be taken with an individual child has been described in detail by Bull and Solity (1987). They outline the following eight-step assessment procedure. (The steps are listed in short form; the explanatory comments are ours.)

Step 1: Ask some pertinent questions. This relates to the emotional effects which difficult behaviour and difficult children can have on the teacher. The teacher should try to decide what it is that is annoying her and whether her judgement is being hampered by extraneous factors such as knowledge of the child's family or the way the child looks.

Step 2: Define the behaviour which is of concern. This is similar to the 'Restate the problem in clear performance terms' step in the problem-solving approach (PSA). It requires the teacher to write down exactly what it is that the child does which causes concern.

Step 3: Observe the behaviour. This is the same as the 'Gathering information' step in the PSA.

Step 4: Compare the child's behaviour with that of his peers. Here the aim is to try to decide how different this child's behaviour is to that of others in his class. It is, in effect, another check on the teacher's own objectivity.

Step 5: Assess the effects of the behaviour. It is useful to gauge what effect the child's behaviour is having both on his own activities and those of his classmates. This is often the deciding factor for teachers, who feel that the behaviour of difficult children has an unjustifiably detrimental effect on the rest of the class.

Step 6: Estimate other pupils' acceptance. The friendship groups which occur in classes can often give some clues as to how well the child is accepted by his peers. Sometimes difficult children are complained about to their teachers but sometimes the difficult behaviour appears not to bother their classmates.

Step 7: Try to identify relevant factors in the environment. This step aims to consider factors within the context of the school and class situation which may be relevant to the difficult behaviour. These may be occurring prior to the behaviour and so may be 'triggering' it. Alternatively, there may be events that follow upon the behaviour and are reinforcing it by rewarding the child in some way.

Step 8: Find out how widespread the difficulties are. This is likely to involve the teacher in talking to colleagues who also know or teach the child. Their perceptions of the child may help in deciding how widespread and how serious a problem it is.

At the end of this process, Bull and Solity suggest, the teacher should summarize her findings along each of the suggested dimensions and then assess the overall seriousness of the behaviour. It may be that this procedure could prove a useful precursor to the problem-solving approach. If, at the end of the eight steps, it is decided that the problem is serious enough to warrant specific action, then applying the PSA would help in deciding what that action should be.

CLASSROOM MANAGEMENT: GOOD PRACTICE

For many newly qualified teachers, how successful their teaching is and how much they enjoy their first post depend very much on the effectiveness of their classroom management. By this we mean how well they manage the children in their class, how well they organize their resources and the layout of the room. There are many texts available to help teachers improve their classroom management; many local authorities run courses, usually involving their Psychological Service or other support agencies, which aim to give practical help in these skills. In this section we will look briefly at some of the areas which are most usually tackled and mention useful texts which can be referred to for more detailed help.

Rules

Most schools have rules. Some of these may be *explicit* and may be found in written form, for instance in a school handbook. More often, there are *implicit* rules, which are imparted to teachers and children alike in a variety of ways and also enforced in a variety of ways. There may be an explicit rule within a school governing walking in the corridors, for example, but implicit rules concerned with movement within a classroom. Alongside a rule there is usually a particular consequence for breaking it, and thus rules differ from *guidelines*, which tend to suggest actions rather than directing them.

Rules are also different from *routines*, which consist of a sequence of actions often initiated by a brief instruction. Examples of routines might be 'going out to play' or 'giving in the books'. There may be some rules associated with these routines: for instance, there may be a 'no running' rule in operation throughout the school, and this would obviously affect the 'going out to play' routine. Rules exist at many different levels in society, and each level of rules must take into account those superordinate rules which are already in place. Thus, there are rules in society (of both a legal and a moral variety) and rules within the home, the LEA and within individual schools. Before the teacher begins to think about the rules she wishes to operate in her classroom she needs to consider those already in existence, particularly the school rules.

The Elton Report (p. 97) recognized the importance of rules within schools and made some suggestions about their formulation:

- Schools should ensure that their rules are derived from principles underlying their behaviour policies.
- Behaviour policies should establish the reasons behind the rules.
- A few pertinent rules are more effective than a long list of prohibitions.

From this it can be seen that the Elton Report viewed the existence of a 'whole-school behaviour policy' as of fundamental importance. The decision to have such a policy depends largely on the senior managers in a school, though other members of staff can exert some influence and can suggest that there would be much to gain from adopting such a scheme. Materials are now available which include in-school courses that lead to the formulation of such policies. Luton *et al.* (1991) have provided a good example of one such practical course.

There are, however, a number of other points which need to be considered when formulating rules within the classroom:

- the rules need to be unambiguous and clearly stated;
- they should be realistic and fair;
- they should be phrased positively, wherever possible;
- the pupils should be involved in the formulation of the rules, if this is possible.

(This latter will ensure that pupils understand the rules as well as the reasons behind them and will have a degree of commitment to making them work.) Any class rules constructed in this way should be reviewed regularly to check that they are still necessary, still appropriate and still being followed.

It is important for the teacher to consider how she is going to communicate the rules to all the people who need to know. This is not difficult when class rules are being considered, but the list of people may be a little longer for school rules. Thus parents and governors, in particular, would benefit from knowing the rules and they, in turn, can help by re-emphasizing the rules to the children as any disciplinary matters arise.

Within any class, there are a variety of ways to ensure that the children remember and understand the rules. It may be that a class assembly can take one of the rules as its theme and a story can be constructed around it. Perhaps the school or class can have a 'rule of the week' which everyone makes an effort to obey. In some classes the rules (usually few in number) are displayed on a poster in the classroom and it is part of the regular class routine to review a rule and its effectiveness.

Rewards

Once the systems of rules and routines are set up within the school and class, it is vital that there is a clear understanding on the part of both children and teachers of what will happen as a consequence of keeping or breaking the rules. Basic psychology tells us that if the consequences of a particular behaviour are rewarding, then the behaviour is more likely to occur again in the future. Conversely, if the consequences of the behaviour are punishing, then the behaviour is less likely to occur in the future.

The Elton Report recommended that schools should endeavour to strike a healthy balance between rewards and punishments and that both should be clearly specified. It is interesting to consider teachers' attitudes to good behaviour and how these compare with their attitudes to good work. Research evidence tends to show that teachers will reward good work but are often reluctant to reward good behaviour, as that is expected and therefore taken for granted. The Elton Report noted that very often pupils in classes can get their teacher's attention in one of two ways: either by working well or by behaving badly. For children with learning difficulties or short concentration spans, it may be that the only way they can get themselves noticed is by misbehaving. Therefore, rewarding good behaviour can produce improvements.

A system which has come to be known as 'Catch 'em being good' uses this technique; the teacher is encouraged to praise appropriate behaviour when she can, rather than pointing out the children who are not doing as they have been asked. With some difficult children it can be quite a skill to spot when they are actually doing as they should and then register some meaningful praise before they reoffend.

If we consider rewarding *improvements* in work and behaviour, rather than the actual standards attained, it has been shown that teachers are happier to reward work improvements, even for work that is below standard but obviously involved an effort, than they are to reward improved behaviour. They still require behaviour to meet a certain standard before they feel justified in rewarding the child. Finally, many teachers feel that rewarding good behaviour, particularly for a child who doesn't always behave well, is not fair on the other children. Why should a child be rewarded for doing what the other children do anyway? It is worth the teacher considering these issues in some depth because they have implications for the rule systems within the class and for how the teacher might handle particular individuals within the class. The rewards employed may need to be flexible enough to allow a variety of personalized rewards where necessary. It is also helpful if the teacher has taken her class along with her in the preliminary discussions. The children might then be able to understand why it is important that every child in the class conforms to the rules. In this way they can both exert some peer pressure on any miscreant and can understand why he might need to be given some intermediary reward in order to help him learn to conform to all the class rules.

Guidelines for using rewards

When choosing rewards to use in the classroom there are a few questions it is pertinent to ask.

Is the reward really a reward?
It is sometimes necessary to check that what is considered a reward by the teacher is actually viewed as such by all the children in a class. An example might be the over-liberal use of praise for some children, particularly older ones.

Is the reward used consistently?
It is important, especially in the early stages of establishing new behaviour patterns, that rewards are used consistently. It is very easy for teachers, during the course of a busy day, to forget what they have said will happen, but children rarely forget, especially when the consequences promised are pleasant!

Is the reward immediate enough?
The most effective rewards, especially for young children, are given immediately after the good behaviour.

Does the child know what he is being rewarded for?
When any reward is given, it should, if possible, be accompanied by a reminder of why the child has earned the reward. This will reinforce the good behaviour in the child but will also remind others in the class of how they should behave and what the rule is.

Are the rewards 'phased out' appropriately?
Some teachers worry that if specific rewards are used then some children will always need and expect them and will not do as asked without them. However, this is not borne out in practice. The aim with most reward systems is that the rewards should be gradually phased out until the child becomes self-rewarded by conforming and enjoying the benefits of behaving well. This phasing out can be achieved in a number of ways;

- by replacing 'strong', tangible rewards, such as stickers or sweets, by less strong rewards, such as praise;
- by raising the standards of work or behaviour to earn the same reward;
- by rewarding less frequently, for instance once a week rather than once a day.

Finally, it is worth remembering that rewards will lose their effect if over-used. Children will become bored and so it is worth having a variety of rewards available so that they can be changed regularly. Although praise can be used to good effect at all times, it is also worth remembering that it is not simply the quantity of praise which is important. Ainscow and Tweddle (1988, p. 60) refer to 'an almost blind faith that simply increasing the amount of praise used by a teacher will improve children's academic progress and social behaviour'. They go on to cite research by Brophy (1983) that recommends teachers to concentrate on praising well rather than praising often. Brophy argues that rewards should only be given for genuine progress and that the aim should always be for children to expend effort because they achieve enjoyment and satisfaction from behaving and working well.

Sanctions

In order to achieve the 'healthy balance' recommended in the Elton Report between rewards and punishments, it is necessary to have a well-defined and easily understood system of sanctions in place as well. Many of the guidelines suggested for rewards are equally applicable to sanctions. Recommendation 24 stated:

> pupils should learn from experience to expect fair and consistently applied punishments for bad behaviour which make the distinction between serious and minor offences apparent.

The Report also noted that more punitive regimes tended to result in worse rather than better behaviour, and so it suggested a positive approach wherever possible.

Let us briefly run through some guidelines for setting up systems of sanctions and for using punishment, whatever form it takes, as effectively as possible.

Is the punishment really a punishment?
In the same way that we recommend a check is made that rewards are rewarding, it is useful to check that a punishment is actually unpleasant for a child. Staying in at breaktime may be undesirable to one child but may be ideal for another as it means he has easy access to all sorts of temptations within the class or school.

Is the punishment applied consistently?
It is important to remember that any threats which are made must be carried out, to ensure that future punishments are effective but also to maintain the teacher's status.

Is the punishment immediate enough?
As with rewards, punishments should ideally be given as soon after the problem behaviour as possible. When circumstances do not allow this, the child should be reminded why he is receiving the punishment at the time it is given.

Does the child know why he is being punished?
Accompanying any punishment should be a brief, clear explanation of what the child has done wrong. This should, where possible, focus on the misdeed and not on the child himself. In other words you should aim to condemn the behaviour and not the child.

Does the punishment fit the crime?
Wherever possible, the punishment should be linked to the crime in a way that allows the culprit in some way to repair the damage, be it to property or to another child. It is also important, as has been mentioned earlier, to discriminate between serious misbehaviours and minor transgressions. Here it may be necessary to employ some of the advice given earlier to decide the seriousness of a problem. The teacher might also need to

examine her own feelings towards the child and the child's behaviour to decide whether or not she is over-reacting.

Is the punishment fair?

This relates to the previous point, but it is worth noting that fairness needs to be apparent to *all* of the class members. The Elton Report suggested that children respond well to the notion of 'fair play'. Therefore, the technique of punishing the innocent with the guilty, as happens when the whole class is kept in until one culprit is found, is not recommended because it is seen as basically unfair by the majority of pupils. The Report also recommends that punishments which seek to humiliate pupils, perhaps by using public ridicule, should not be used as this makes re-establishing good relationships with the child almost impossible.

Is the punishment applied calmly?

It is better for both children and teachers if punishments are administered calmly by teachers. It is less stressful for the teacher and usually more effective from the child's point of view.

It is difficult to give advice on types of sanctions. They vary from school to school, and individual teachers do seem to have their favourites. Since the abolition of corporal punishment in British schools, teachers and heads have been forced to become more creative in the range of sanctions that they use. Most have found that they have not missed being able to use that 'ultimate sanction' and they see its abolition as a good thing. As a general rule, it is best to use as modest a punishment as will be effective. Do not use your strongest sanctions for petty crimes or for first offences. Make sure you have a hierarchy of sanctions available, even if they are only in your head! These guidelines, along with those offered for using rewards, are described with accompanying activities for teachers to try, in Luton *et al.* (1991).

CLASSROOM ORGANIZATION

There are many texts which give advice on how to organize the classroom in order to achieve the most effective learning and teaching. Research has considered whether or not children learn better sitting in rows or grouped around tables. Basically, it seems that seating arrangements should be governed by what the teacher hopes to achieve from the lesson. Thus, if the aim is for co-operative work with discussion between two or more children, then the children need to be grouped accordingly. For tasks which require the children to concentrate and to stay on the particular task in hand for a sustained length of time, then it is better for the children to sit as far apart as possible or to sit in mixed-up social groupings.

Seating all the children who have learning difficulties together or all the children who cause behavioural difficulties together is a recipe for disaster. Standards of behaviour and work will drop. Many teachers find it useful to have children who are being particularly difficult sitting near to their base. Others prefer to tuck them away in a corner, to lower the distraction levels for the other children. Another tactic is to sit them with their backs to the rest of the class – but beware of putting them in front of a window! This usually ensures no work at all from the isolated children.

The best guideline is to experiment within the class to ensure that the arrangements made are achieving their intended outcome. In other words, if a child is moved as a punishment, the teacher should ensure that he is not finding the move rewarding. Nor is it a good idea to seat a child who is presenting behavioural difficulties, but is also socially isolated and beginning to show aggression to the other children, permanently at a distance from his peers.

The introduction of the National Curriculum has obliged teachers to consider their grouping and seating strategies more closely. Many of the Attainment Targets within the National Curriculum require children to work co-operatively on tasks, particularly in such areas as Science. In addition, to be able to undertake the required on-going assessments, teachers need to circulate between groups checking the children's understanding by talking to them about the tasks in hand. In these ways curriculum requirements govern the arrangements for seating and the organization of resources.

RESOURCES

As we saw in the example of the problem-solving approach (pp. 78–80), resources can be either a hindrance or an aid in the way they influence children's behaviour in the classroom. It is therefore worth giving some time, both at the start of term when resources are arranged in the class and also regularly throughout the term, to consider:

- the best places to store limited resources;
- how children are allowed to access resources;
- what resources need to be available to each child or group of children.

If the system is sensible and efficient, not requiring a great deal of queuing or unlocking of cupboards, then the whole business of accessing resources becomes routine and does not detract from the teaching and learning process.

PERSONAL TEACHING SKILLS

Personal teaching skills include non-verbal skills, such as eye contact, voice modulation, posture and positioning around the classroom.

There are many textbooks that seek to help teachers improve these skills, and give exercises to try in the classroom. They also consider factors which can enhance a teacher's status in the eyes of their pupils and so make classroom management of behavioural difficulties a little easier.

Kounin, writing in 1970, looked at teacher characteristics that encourage pupils to keep busy and so reduce behaviour problems. He highlighted 'teacher with-it-ness' as an important factor. By this he meant the ability to know what is happening all around the classroom and to make all the children aware of their teacher's presence at all times.

He also identified 'overlappingness', by which he meant the ability to attend to more than one thing at a time. Anyone who has tried to teach in a busy primary school classroom will know that this is an essential skill. Unfortunately, not everyone has it naturally and some people need to work on it harder than others.

Another essential factor, in Kounin's view, is 'momentum': the skill of being able to keep the lesson sufficiently interesting for all children (so the brighter children are not 'treading water') while, at the same time, supervising and managing the necessary changes of activity and movement around the classroom. As we mentioned earlier, good resource organization will help in this.

Finally, Kounin stressed the importance of 'group-alerting': the skill of keeping the children's attention by adding elements of surprise and suspense to the lessons. It also entails gaining their co-operation by making them aware that they are accountable for their work and might be called upon to participate in the lesson at any time.

These are just a few factors, associated with teacher behaviour, which can improve overall classroom management and so make dealing with any behaviour problems, be they small or large, a little easier.

INDIVIDUAL CHILDREN PRESENTING BEHAVIOUR PROBLEMS

We have outlined the effectiveness of the problem-solving approach (pp. 73–8) in helping to analyse problems and decide not only what a child is doing wrong but also how to aim at specific improvements. We have also discussed how to use rewards and punishments effectively. Both these are important techniques for encouraging behaviour change. There are a few specific techniques which can be used with individual primary-age children.

Home–school books

We often refer to the value of involving parents; their help can be vital in trying to tackle behaviour problems. One way to elicit their support is to set up a home–school book for written messages between home and school on a regular basis. The teacher's messages should, wherever possible, be positive; for example, suggesting ideas for improvement. Obviously this technique will not work for homes where English is not read, perhaps not even spoken. In such cases sensitivity and a little creativity will be needed to circumvent the problem.

Daily report systems

Daily report systems can be used either to improve specific behaviours or to monitor the child's overall performance. They are more effective if parents are involved in the process, perhaps as a minimum by signing the report card on a weekly basis. Any report system should be used for a specified length of time and the aim should be to phase it out when possible.

Contracts

Contracts are along the same lines as the previous techniques but put matters on a more formal basis. Contracts are becoming more and more popular with teachers both in primary and secondary schools, probably because of their very individualized nature and the fact that in a contract everyone's role is clearly defined. In Luton *et al.* (1991, p. 37), a contract is defined as:

> a negotiated agreement between the pupil, school (and often parents) about the rewards and privileges which the pupil can earn for maintaining certain specified standards of behaviour. The agreed actions of the pupil and adult parties are written down formally and signed.

Home–school books, daily reports or contracts can form part of a PSA action plan.

Self-reporting and self-monitoring

For older or more mature children, using self-reporting as a tool can be very effective. Teacher and child devise a self-report form to cover the areas of concern, or they can use one of a range of published self-report checklists. Useful examples are contained in Appendix 3 of Wolfendale's book (1987).

There are numerous other techniques (Sprick, 1981) which can be of value, depending on the ages of the children and the nature of the difficulties and, as long as they are employed in a responsible and methodical way, with the teacher monitoring their effectiveness. It is best for each teacher to try out and then to adopt whichever suits her needs best.

CHAPTER SUMMARY

In this chapter we outlined and gave examples of the problem-solving approach, which we argued was sufficiently adaptable and sufficiently proven to be recommended for use in schools. We pointed to the advantages of this approach in helping teachers to prioritize their concerns and to choose a suitable area on which to work. We recommended a set of guidelines which can help teachers in deciding on the seriousness of the problems which occur in their classrooms. Other factors that influence children's behaviour were addressed, such as classroom management, including the use of rules, rewards and sanctions, the organization of the classroom, the use of resources. Finally, we highlighted some aspects of personal teaching skills. The message throughout was that good classroom practice will make the teaching of *all* children more efficient and effective as well as preventing unnecessary disruption by individuals.

Our final section applied the problem-solving approach to individual children and suggested some techniques which might be considered as part of action plans: home–school books, daily report systems, contracts and self-monitoring systems.

SUGGESTIONS FOR FURTHER READING

Cheeseman, P. and Watts, P. (1985) *Positive Behaviour Management: A Manual for Teachers*. Beckenham: Croom Helm. A short, readable text with very specific guidance for implementing individual programmes.

Grunsell, R. (1985) *Finding Answers to Disruption*. Harlow: Longman/Schools Council. A set of ideas and activities which, although secondary-school-based, provide approaches to difficult behaviour that will be useful to teachers in primary schools.

Luton, K., Booth, G., Leadbetter, J., Tee, G. and Wallace, F. (1991) *Positive Strategies for Behaviour Management*. Windsor: NFER-Nelson. A pack of INSET materials for use in primary schools, covering topics such as 'School organization' and 'Involving parents in behaviour difficulties'.

Robertson, J. (1981) *Effective Classroom Control*. Sevenoaks: Hodder & Stoughton. A text which considers some of the important non-verbal aspects of teaching performance.

Westmacott, E. V. S. and Cameron, R. J. (1983) *Behaviour Can Change*. London: Macmillan. A well-written and often amusing short text which gives the basics of behaviour modification in a digestible form.

Wragg, E. C. (1981) *Classroom Management and Control*. A workbook containing exercises particularly geared to help teachers in the early stages of building up relationships with classes of children.

CHAPTER 7

Other groups of children with special educational needs

CHAPTER OVERVIEW

This chapter focuses on six groups of children who have special educational needs: the hearing-impaired, the visually impaired, those with physical disabilities, those with severe learning difficulties, those exhibiting autistic features and finally those with language and communication delays and disorders. Some of the children are mainly educated in mainstream schools and some exclusively in special settings. We aim to provide brief information about each group and to explore some of the issues surrounding their education, including the implications for teachers of integrating these special needs children in mainstream classrooms.

HEARING IMPAIRMENT

General information

The two types of deafness that affect children are very different in terms of their causes, levels of hearing loss and prognoses. The first, *conductive deafness* (otitis media or secretory otitis), is a relatively common condition in young children up to the age of 7 years, affecting 1 in 4 or 5 children. It is caused by sound not being properly transmitted to the eardrum because of a blockage in the ear canal due to the build-up of fluid (maybe because of a heavy cold, infection or catarrh) or of wax in the middle ear. As these conditions can vary in severity from hour to hour and as the thickness of the liquid in the ear can change dramatically, the child may experience extreme variations in the overall volume of sound that he hears.

Owing to the intermittent nature of such a loss, a child may not be identified during a routine test as having any difficulties. Thus it is important for teachers, who are in regular, close contact with children, to be aware of signs which may indicate a hearing loss (see p. 96). It is usually possible to treat the condition with medication but sometimes surgery is necessary. This involves the child being fitted with grommets: tiny plastic tubes inserted into the eardrum that help to drain off the fluid and equalize the pressure on both sides of the drum. The grommets eventually drop out by themselves.

The second, more serious, form of hearing impairment is known as *sensori-neural deafness*. This is a far less common condition, with approximately one in 1000 children being affected. It is a permanent loss resulting from irreversible damage to the nerve endings of the inner ear. Causes include hereditary factors, adverse prenatal conditions (especially maternal rubella, i.e. German measles), adverse conditions around the time of the birth (perinatal factors) and some post-natal conditions, the most common being meningitis.

The degree of hearing loss due to this form of deafness can be moderate but is more usually severe (71–95 decibels) or profound (96 decibels or more). It is sometimes in one ear only (monaural) but more usually affects both ears (binaural). There is no medical cure, but the use of hearing aids can enhance any residual hearing. There are four main types of hearing aid which are used by children: body-worn aids, behind-the-ear aids (often referred to as post-aural aids), in-the-ear aids and radio hearing aids. Unfortunately many hearing aids amplify all the sounds in a room, so the child may receive a high level of interference from the background noise in a typical primary classroom, making the teacher's voice difficult to distinguish. The problem can be minimized, to a certain extent, by fitting the child with a radio hearing aid. This requires the teacher to wear a small microphone and the child a small radio receiver. In this way the teacher's voice is amplified instead of all the other noises or voices. However, this can cause problems in itself, as we shall see later on in the section on teaching implications.

Issues of integration

Recent statistics published by the National Deaf Children's Society (1987) show that of an estimated 28,000 school-aged children with significant hearing impairments, 14 per cent are educated in special schools for the deaf, 15 per cent in units in ordinary schools (usually with the support of qualified teachers of the deaf) and 71 per cent in their local mainstream schools, with varying levels of support from visiting teachers of the deaf, who are usually employed by the local education authority. The levels of integration vary between authorities, depending on the availability of other types of provision and upon the levels of support available to mainstream schools. Some of the units attached to mainstream schools, a popular form of provision in many authorities, practise varying degrees of integration from the unit to the main school. As we have mentioned in Chapter 2, the success of such integration will depend to a great extent on the attitudes of all the staff in the school.

As mentioned above, most children suffering from a conductive loss are educated in mainstream or unit provision. There are various kinds of support available to such children. Visiting (peripatetic) teachers of the hearing-impaired may visit individual children on a regular basis. Their functions will include checking that hearing aids are set correctly, are clean and in good working order. They may periodically review the child's hearing by performing tests to check that there has been no change in the levels of loss. They will also provide advice to the class teacher on a range of matters. Within units all the above services can be provided but there are usually trained teachers of the deaf available to teach and to advise staff.

The trend towards integration of hearing-impaired children into mainstream schools has gained particular support because of the high success rates, both in terms of children's educational attainments and their social relations. It is particularly advantageous for children with hearing impairment to be in a normal, verbal/vocal environment as it gives them maximum exposure to spoken language. (This is assuming that adequate support for their overall educational needs is available.) For some children, however, a school for the deaf remains the most appropriate option. Many schools for deaf children attain extremely high standards of academic work and some schools are able to cater for children having multiple difficulties, deafness being one of them.

Decisions about placements are often dependent on the preferred mode of communication of the school or provision (i.e. verbal or signed). There is a long-running, often heated, debate as to which mode of communication is most beneficial. The 'oralists' believe that the main aim should be to help children to speak with as close a proximation to normal speech as is possible. They argue that in this way the children will be 'normalized' and so able to communicate with others around them, even though, in many cases, it will be in a severely limited fashion.

There are those, on the other hand, who argue that the child's powers of communication should be developed and enhanced by teaching him to use a signed communication system. Advocates of this approach maintain that systems such as British Sign Language (BSL) are complete languages. They advocate that all deaf children should be taught a signed system in order that they can develop their own thought and language systems as far as they are able, without being restricted to whatever they are able to hear and speak orally. Most schools for the deaf have teachers who are competent signers, whereas this approach is much less viable in a typical primary school.

An approach that seeks to combine aspects of both options is called 'total communication'.

Total communication

Signs are introduced as a supplement to speech with the idea of accelerating the acquisition of verbal language by utilizing the child's vision. Some special schools use this approach and are achieving positive results with children. One significant factor in deciding whether or not a child should be taught to sign is whether either or both of the parents are deaf. If this is the case and if the parent already signs regularly, then it will obviously be beneficial for the child to learn to sign. In this way communication between the child and his parents will be enhanced.

Teaching implications

Many teachers in primary schools will find that they have a child in their class with some degree of hearing loss. If the loss is significant, then it is likely that some level of support will be provided by specialist visiting teachers. However, there may be other children with slight or intermittent hearing losses for whom there is no identified form of support. It is therefore important for every class teacher to be aware of and informed about children with hearing impairment.

Identification

There are a number of factors which may indicate that a child is having difficulties with his or her hearing. None, in isolation, *necessarily* means that the child is suffering from such a condition; in fact, they may indicate problems in other areas. They do indicate, however, that the teacher should be alerted and begin to check out other aspects of the child's work and behaviour. The first and most common occurrence is that the child has *speech problems*. Mispronunciation and confusion of sounds are two possible problems, but more likely is the omission of various parts of words, particularly the beginnings or endings. Another pointer is *inattention in class*, particularly during activities which most children enjoy (e.g. storytime). A third (which may seem obvious but is open to various interpretations by teachers) is a *failure to respond when spoken to* or *responding inappropriately*. A further indicator, particularly for older children, might be *poor results in dictation work*, particularly where other results are good. *Close watching of a speaker's face* is also important as it might indicate a reliance on lip-reading. *Turning the head to one side, when listening* may indicate that a child is consciously or unconsciously turning to use his stronger ear to best effect. Finally, a more unusual but important sign might be the use of *abnormal language structures*. Should any of these occur persistently or in combination then the teacher should pursue the matter further.

Room adaptation and seating

Classrooms are generally noisy places. Acoustically, they can make life very difficult for the hearing-impaired child, especially as hearing aids often pick up and amplify background noise. Therefore, any room adaptations which can improve the acoustics and absorb background or incidental sounds should be made. Carpets can greatly reduce the sounds of chairs and tables scraping as children get out of their seats. Curtains, pinboards and acoustic tiles can also cut down incidental noise.

If such adaptations cannot be made at once, then it is important to seat a child with hearing difficulties away from any persistent noise, e.g. the classroom door, the stock cupboard, the gerbils. Another seating consideration is the position of the light source. If a child needs to observe the teacher's movements, gestures and lips, then he should not be seated looking directly into a light source, such as the window. It would be ideal, other considerations allowing, to seat him so that light from the window can illuminate the teacher and blackboard, or other teaching aid. If the child's hearing is better on one side than the other, then the teacher should ensure that the better ear is nearest to her. Also, it is necessary to ensure that the child can turn round easily to observe other members of the class talking when group discussions are taking place.

Communication

There are some features of the teacher's language and management style which, if attention is paid to them, can greatly help the hearing-impaired child.

- During oral work, ensure that the pace of the discussion is not too fast for the child to follow.

- Make sure that the child can view all members of the class and point to the child who is speaking to help the hearing-impaired child to locate the sound.
- Repeat and rephrase the answers that other children give because the teacher's voice will be better amplified and more familiar to the child.
- Sensitize the other children in the class to the needs of the hearing-impaired child, particularly with regard to the fact that there will be a time delay in answering questions.
- Remember that the child will lose all visual clues under blackout conditions, such as when filmstrips, slides or videos are shown. At these times the child may need to be moved closer to the teacher for extra help.
- Be aware that using an overhead projector can be problematic. The teacher is often talking while using this visual resource. The noise of the fan may affect the hearing aid of a hearing-impaired child, and lip-reading is impossible in the dark or if the teacher is facing away.
- For tackling written work, glossaries and vocabulary lists can be useful in aiding the child's understanding of the content.
- Explain the purpose of handouts before they are distributed, then allow reading time before continuing with the lesson.
- Tell the child of any changes in routine personally, in case he missed the general announcements, otherwise he may be unduly frightened by events such as fire drills.
- Repeat notices that were given in assembly for the benefit of the class as a whole but for the hearing-impaired child in particular.

VISUAL IMPAIRMENT

General information

There are many different conditions which can cause visual impairment in children. Some are severe and some milder but many are correctable, as long as they are identified and correctly diagnosed. For simplicity's sake we consider the problems under four headings, but it must be remembered that children may have to cope with a combination of defects.

Focusing problems

Focusing problems are the most common defect and can, in the main, be corrected by spectacles or other aids to vision. If a child suffers from a focusing problem, then his visual acuity, or the sharpness of the visual image he perceives, is affected. To test whether this is a problem at a distance, the commonly known optician's chart (or Snellen chart) is used, with letters of diminishing size displayed. The result of the test is written as one number over the other. Normal vision might be written as 6/6, meaning that the person can see at 6 metres that which should be seen at 6 metres with normal sight. 6/18 means that a person sees at 6 metres what should normally be seen at 18 metres and hence the person has quite a severe visual difficulty. At least 6/12 vision is needed to drive.

Near-vision problems are measured using the 'N-print test', which indicates the size of print a child can comfortably read at an optimum distance. Secondary textbooks use approximately N. 10 print while initial reading books in infant schools would be N. 18 or greater.

The common terms for these types of problem are short-sightedness (or myopia) if a person's near vision is normal but he has problems seeing objects at a distance and long-sightedness (or hypermetropia) if a person's distance vision is normal but he has difficulty focusing on nearby objects.

There are official definitions of *blind* and *partial sight* which lead to the person being registered and so entitled to magnifiers and other visual aids and sometimes to financial help from local or central government and voluntary agencies or charities. Partial sight is vision that ranges, after correction, from 6/18 to 6/60. A person is generally regarded as blind if his visual acuity is below 3/60 in both eyes or 6/60 with a restricted field of vision.

Field defects

A child may suffer from *peripheral* visual problems, which means that the sight at the outer edges of his field of vision is restricted in some way. Alternately, he may have *central field* problems, meaning that he may have blind spots that encumber his vision. *Cataracts*, which are a build-up of opaque layers on the lens of the eye, are a major cause of such problems.

Eye movement disorders

Some children suffer from *nystagmus*, which is an involuntary oscillation of the eyes which hinders their focusing and accurate tracking. Visual tracking is when a person's eyes follow the progress of an object across the field of vision. A second condition in this category is a *squint*, which occurs when the visual axes of the eyes are not straight: one eye turns in or out. The effect is that the child suffers from double vision. A squint can usually be successfully treated before the child is six by corrective surgery.

Colour blindness

The most common problem in this category is a red–green confusion. To the child, both colours appear greyish. The condition may be diffi-cult to detect as children tend to find ways of compensating for any problems that occur. (They may use other visual clues when colour matching or sorting.) It is much more common in males than females, with an estimated 10 per cent of the male population being affected. It is extremely rare for a person to be totally colour blind.

Issues of integration

The question of integration for a visually impaired child depends largely on the severity of the child's condition and the range of provi-sion available within the local authority. For children with a severe visual impairment, it is likely that they will need to be taught to read Braille. Therefore they will need plenty of materials written in Braille, access to equipment such as a Brailler, low-vision aids and, not least, the help of a trained teacher of the visually impaired. In a number of authorities this level of resourcing is only available in a school for the blind and partially sighted, and for many children this is an appropriate environment. Some schools have units or resource bases for children with visual difficulties which can provide specialist teaching and appropriate equipment. Increasingly, many children with lesser difficulties are supported in this way, which provides many opportunities for real integration.

Finally, some children can be maintained in their local primary school with minimal adaptations, such as blinds at the window to cut out glare (necessary for children who are sensitive to light or *photo-phobic*). If support is available from specialist visiting teachers of the visually impaired, then many children can benefit enormously from being with their sighted peers.

In mainstream primary schools which do integrate visually impaired children, some adaptations to the school as a whole may need to be undertaken. Any stairs or individual steps may need to be painted or have bright strips stuck on them to make sure they stand out. Glass doors should be made more visible by putting posters or luminous tape on them. There should be no obstacles in corridors and in crowded areas. Movements around the school should, wherever possible, be controlled either by tight supervision or by instituting rules, such as 'walk on the left'.

Teaching implications

In every primary school class there will be some children wearing spectacles. Usually, this means that their visual difficulty has been detected, diagnosed and the correct spectacles prescribed for them. It is important for the teacher to know when the child should be wearing the spectacles (i.e. for all activities or just for close-up work) and also to check their condition. Many children are very self-conscious about wearing glasses and invent ploys in order to be rid of them. Teachers should beware of perpetual excuses. There may also be children in class who have an undetected visual problem and so, as with hearing-impaired children, it is vital that the mainstream class teacher is well-informed and vigilant.

Identification

Signs that a child may have a visual difficulty may include the following:

- head positioned unusually close to or distant from work;
- poor handwriting or poor hand–eye co-ordination;
- clumsy in physical activities, bumping into things, etc.;
- obvious discomfort in bright light;
- inaccurate copying from the board or books;
- writing through, rather than on, lines;
- non-closure of letters;
- not appearing to look at the person to whom he is talking.

In any such case the child's vision should be investigated further, either by referral to the school's medical officer or by the child's parents taking him to their local doctor.

Associated learning factors

If a child has a substantial visual defect, then his experience of the world is likely to be more limited than that of his peers. This may cause significant gaps in his knowledge; misconceptions or inadequate understanding of his environment. Consequently, on some educational tasks he may well perform less well than his sighted peers, but this may not be a true reflection of his ability.

Visually impaired children may, in some cases, develop at a slightly slower rate than sighted children. Thus, a child entering infant school may have developed the skill of reaching out and locating an object much later than other children. He may therefore need to be given more time to experience the handling of a variety of objects. In terms of his intellectual development, the concept of object permanence (the realization that objects and people continue to exist even when they are out of sight) may well arrive at between three and five years rather than at the normal age of about two. This may well have implications for early school experiences. For instance, the child may be especially distressed by separation from carers or favourite objects.

Another outcome of limited vision may be that the child cannot see clearly the non-verbal signals that people use to convey meaning, or the facial expressions of encouragement, interest, boredom or irritation. Thus the child could seem anti-social or lacking in social skills, if he fails to respond appropriately to others.

Management

For most children with a significant visual difficulty who remain in mainstream school, practical advice and guidance should be provided from trained teachers of the visually impaired. This is because visual problems vary so much that general rules do not always apply. However, the following factors should always be given consideration.

The amount of light available will vary across the classroom, making *seating* an important consideration. Some children may require enhanced lighting whereas others, as we have seen earlier, definitely do not. In all cases, however, it is important to allow the child freedom to approach the blackboard and other wall-mounted materials. The *height and type of desk and chair* are important, particularly the adjustability and reflective nature of the desk. *Blackboards* should be black, rather than green or grey, and should be thoroughly cleaned. *Reading materials* should be chosen to avoid schemes where print is laid over illustrations. If possible, use good spacing and clear type on matt white paper.

It is vital that class teachers remember that, as with many children with special needs but more particularly those with a visual impairment, work involving reading or recording in any form will take longer. Therefore it is important to make allowances for such individual differences in terms of preparation, lesson planning and classroom management.

PHYSICAL DIFFICULTIES

General information

Many of the major handicapping conditions which affect children are serious and disabling, and so mean that the child's educational life will be spent wholly in a special school. However, in some schools, the integration of a range of children with physical difficulties is successfully accomplished and so it will be useful to mention these conditions, however briefly.

The first condition which affects children both mildly and severely is *cerebral palsy*. This is a disorder of movement or posture which is due to malfunction of, or damage to, the brain. Some children with mild cerebral palsy (or CP, as it is often known) are not affected intellectually at all and may only be affected in their fine motor skills or gait. Other, more severe, cases may fall into one of three classifications which group children according to the predominant movement disorder. These are *spasticity*, where limb muscles are tight, causing excessive contraction and jerkiness of movement; *athetosis*, characterized by involuntary, purposeless movements; and *ataxia*, in which condition the child has little sense of balance and so makes uncoordinated movements. Children who suffer from CP may have associated problems. Typically, these may be difficulties with swallowing, which results in drooling, and speech disorders, hearing loss or sight defects.

Spina bifida and *hydrocephalus* are conditions which commonly occur together but can occur in isolation. The former is a congenital abnormality in which one or more of the spinal vertebrae have failed to fuse together so that the spine is split in two. The latter occurs when excess fluid builds up within the brain. Approximately two-thirds of the children who have spina bifida also have hydrocephalus.

There are other physical conditions which affect groups of children and which will have a bearing on their educational needs. These include *cystic fibrosis*, which is an inherited disease mainly affecting the lungs and the digestive system. Many children with this condition can be maintained in mainstream education with minimal medical back-up to ensure their medication is taken regularly. *Muscular dystrophy* is also an inherited progressive neuro-muscular disease. There are different forms of the condition, but the most common, Duchenne-type, affects only boys, although the defective gene is carried through the female line. The condition is characterized by a degeneration of muscle cells and a consequent weakening of the limbs. Many children with this disease can remain within mainstream education, provided resources and support are available. However, transfer to a more specialized environment may be necessary as the disease progresses.

Epilepsy and *asthma* are two conditions which can be debilitating when they occur but do not usually prevent children from benefiting from mainstream education. Usually epilepsy has been identified before the child enters school, and so staff can be alerted to the precautions that need to be taken. The types of epileptic fit or seizure can vary both in form and severity. They range from a minor fit or 'petit mal' which is often characterized by the child staring blankly and frequently blinking his eyes, to a major fit or 'grand mal' convulsion. The latter can be disturbing to onlookers, especially if they have not witnessed such a fit before, and potentially dangerous to the child, depending on the situation in which it occurs and the assistance provided. In the case of children who have major fits staff should be forewarned and should ensure that they know how to provide or where to seek appropriate assistance. However, it is relatively easy for teachers to be trained to cope with fits.

Asthma is one of the most commonly occurring diseases of childhood. There is evidence to suggest that its incidence is increasing, possibly because of the higher levels of environmental pollution. In most children asthma appears as laboured, wheezy breathing caused by a temporary spasm of the breathing tubes. When it is severe it can be quite distressing for the child. Attacks may be brought on by a number of factors, the most common being allergic reactions. Other causes are viral infections, physical exertion and emotional or psychological upset. Although there is no direct link between asthma and a child's educational progress, if the attacks are severe they may cause the child's health to suffer overall and therefore his performance in school may decline. Additionally, frequent or prolonged attacks may result in a high level of absence from school, which may affect the child's educational progress.

Issues of integration

The integration of children with physical difficulties into mainstream education has occurred across Britain to greater or lesser degrees. Many children within the categories mentioned above are of normal intellectual ability and have much to gain from being with their able-bodied peers. Often, however, the costs of adaptations to the physical environments of schools, such as installing lifts, ramps, changing facilities and wider doorways, have meant that local education authorities have had to select certain schools and to direct children to attend these locally based, specially adapted schools. This system works well as long as the numbers of disabled children are not too great and they are not all clustered together in particular classes. If this happens the benefits of being with a more representative group of children are reduced.

In rural areas the distances involved in transporting children to special schools can sometimes be so great that it is in everyone's best interests for adaptations to be made to a nearby school. However, if a child needs regular or specialized inputs, such as daily physiotherapy, access to a hydrotherapy pool or specialized medical supervision, then these needs may take precedence and the child will attend a special school.

Increasingly, local special schools for children with physical disabilites are providing outreach support to mainstream schools. This can take the form of therapists (e.g. speech therapists or physiotherapists), who are sometimes based in special schools, spending part of their time in supporting children in mainstream settings. Alternatively, specialist teachers can go in to mainstream classes to advise and support those regular class teachers who have disabled children within their groups. This is particularly useful if specialist equipment is being used, such as adapted computers or keyboard, or if special precautions need to be taken for a child during PE lessons or practical activities.

Some authorities employ assistants in schools to look after the physical needs of children, thereby enabling them to have access to the total learning environment. These assistants are called by various titles, e.g. special needs assistants (SNAs), integration assistants, nursery nurses. Some are specially trained but the majority are not and are employed specifically to support one child, or a number of children in one school. They may be needed to change a child, to help him to go to the toilet, to push his wheelchair down the corridor or to supervise him at playtime.

Many children who suffer from a physically disabling condition and whose intellectual functioning is unaffected may have difficulties acquiring certain skills as a consequence of impoverished experience. In the same way that sensorily impaired children are restricted in their early exploratory play days, physically disabled children will have missed out on a range of sensations and opportunities. It is important that teachers of these children are aware of this and so aim to compensate, wherever possible, by providing a range of opportunities and experiences to facilitate their learning.

Some studies have shown that children with physical difficulties are more likely to suffer from *emotional problems* than able-bodied children. This is understandable, as they can often be under strain to keep up with their classmates but may well be unable to talk about the specific effects of their particular problem and how it makes them feel, both physically and emotionally. If possible, pastoral support should be available for these children. For older children, counselling may be desirable but may also be difficult to obtain. Within primary school classes it will often be the child's class teacher who is closest to the child in school and who gets to know his particular times of weakness when he needs understanding and support. Physically disabled children can tire easily and teachers will need to allow for this in their expectations of the child.

Teaching implications

The range of physical problems which affect children is so varied that it is impossible to give specific advice which will be applicable to all children. Teachers should seek out information about any children in their class who have physical difficulties, if it is not readily available to them. They should also identify their main sources of specialist support and advice, and seek direct help and advice. Such a source will often be the local special school for pupils with physical disabilities.

Although most children will have had their condition identified and diagnosed before school age, occasionally some do slip through the net, or initially have mild conditions that become worse and so more obvious. It is therefore important for class teachers to be aware of any children who are particularly *clumsy* or who have very *poor gross motor co-ordination*. This will be most noticeable in PE and games or in the playground. Sometimes physiotherapy can help with mild problems and it is therefore important that potential problems are identified and appropriate referrals made as soon as possible. Similarly, a child may have very *poor fine motor skills*. This may mean that the child has problems with pencil control, manipulating objects, using scissors or completing tasks involving hand–eye co-ordination. Again it is worth asking for a medical opinion because the child may benefit from the advice and support of an occupational therapist or specialist teacher.

For all children with any degree of motor difficulty it is important to find out whether the child is in any pain and whether he takes any medication to alleviate the pain. Flexibility, in terms of the child's seating position, type of chair, the amount and type of work he is asked to produce and the tools or apparatus he is given to use, will help him to fit into the life of the group and gain maximum benefit from being in a normal primary class.

MENTAL HANDICAP (SEVERE LEARNING DIFFICULTIES)

General information

It is only relatively recently that children suffering from a mental handicap were deemed to be the responsibility of local education authorities. The Education Act of 1970 ruled that all children, without exception, should be educated, so this group of children, who had previously been the responsibility of health authorities, came under the jurisdiction of LEAs for the first time. The change provided a challenge to educationalists because existing teaching techniques and curricula were totally unsuitable for children previously deemed 'ineducable'. Schools for ESN(S) – Educationally Sub Normal (Severe) – children were established and these still exist, albeit in a developed form, and are known as SLD schools: schools for children with Severe Learning Difficulties.

Although mental handicap can occur for a number of reasons, notably as a result of cerebral palsy, the largest single cause of mental handicap is *Down's syndrome* and so for this reason the syndrome is worth some consideration. Down's syndrome is a chromosomal abnormality which arises at the time of conception and, unfortunately, there is no cure for it. There is a wide ability range among children who have this condition. Some will have severe learning difficulties and will require high levels of help and support to acquire very basic skills. At the other end of the spectrum, there are children who can function well in a mainstream environment and who can go on to perform useful jobs with a little support or supervision. It is therefore important to guard against low expectations when teaching Down's syndrome children and to ensure that accurate assessments of the child's skills and progress levels are made.

Often children with Down's syndrome may have associated hearing problems, visual problems or, during adolescence, suffer from hypothyroidism. The latter results in the child becoming lethargic and being susceptible to the cold. There are physical features which are common to most children with Down's syndrome; these include shorter than average stature, small head, ears and nose, shortened neck, hands and feet and a small mouth, sometimes resulting in a protruding tongue. This final feature accounts for some of the speech problems experienced by these children.

Issues of integration

Children who are mentally handicapped are usually educated in special schools for children with severe learning difficulties. These schools provide a different type of curriculum as compared with mainstream schools in that the targets and objectives they work towards tend to follow a *developmental sequence*. This means that they try to teach skills in the same general order as they would be acquired in a child developing through the usual sequence of stages. The curriculum is highly structured, with very small steps being tackled in each curriculum area and an emphasis on repetition and reward. There is usually a high priority given to the teaching of life skills and self-help skills. The school necessarily needs to provide a protected environment for many of the children, who will always require high levels of care and supervision.

Some children with lesser degrees of mental impairment may well be maintained in special schools for children with moderate learning difficulties. These were called ESN(M) schools (Educationally Sub-Normal – Moderate) but now tend to be referred to as schools for children with learning difficulties. In these schools the curriculum more closely follows that of mainstream schools, namely the National

Curriculum, but at lower levels. Thus more time is spent on the acquisition of basic skills in academic subjects, and in practical, social and self-help skills. Class sizes are smaller and there is more scope for individual and small-group teaching. Children with Down's syndrome are often placed in this type of school if they are able to cope with the academic work and social demands.

Over the past ten years, and particularly since the 1981 Education Act came into force in 1983, we have seen many more children with moderate learning difficulties and with Down's syndrome being supported in mainstream schools. There are obvious benefits for Down's syndrome children who are placed in primary classes in terms of their language skills, their socialization and the 'normalizing' influence of their peers. If the child can cope with day-to-day modified classroom work, with whatever help is provided, then the placement can be maintained for many years. Some children, however, are able to cope at infant level where a percentage of the work is play-oriented and when their language and early reading skills may be developing apace with that of the others in their class. On entering the junior years, where teaching becomes more formal (in some settings) and when curriculum demands increase, it is sometimes the case that the integrated Down's syndrome child cannot cope with the demands of the class even with high levels of help, so that an alternative placement has to be sought.

Teaching implications

If a child with a degree of mental handicap is integrated into a primary classroom, then it is likely that support will be provided for that child. The type and amount of support will vary from authority to authority but is likely to be either extra teacher time or classroom assistant time. This time may be used to prepare resources especially for that child or in providing extra help and attention during normal lessons and sometimes even in the playground. As we have seen (pp. 38–41), children with learning difficulties will need to follow the same curriculum but broken down into much smaller steps and with high levels of practice built into their programmes of work. Having individual help in the class is invaluable for children who may need instructions repeated several times, who require help to complete set tasks and who respond to high levels of praise.

For class teachers who have classroom assistants or extra teacher time for this purpose, a new set of skills need to be developed. The skills of working collaboratively, in some cases planning and preparing a scheme of work for someone else to deliver and ensuring that the individual child is receiving a balanced and appropriate curriculum, are skills which will need to be acquired or developed by teachers.

Time spent on planning work and ensuring that the child in question benefits, wherever possible, from the topics the whole class are tackling will be beneficial in the long run.

It may be that some tasks are easier to teach in a small group, rather than on an individual basis and so the assistant may take a regular group, including the child with special needs. A good example of this is language development work. Very often the language skills of a child with Down's syndrome are delayed and he needs plenty of exposure to spoken language, which will undoubtedly occur in a mainstream primary classroom! Some structured work is also necessary to ensure that the child's vocabulary is continually increased and that he can use a range of phrase and sentence structures. This can be achieved with regular small-group work, as long as the work is well structured and planned ahead. Apart from being beneficial for the special needs child, it can be very rewarding for a class teacher to have a 'special' child in the class and to see what can be achieved. Finally, for the reasons discussed in Chapter 2, it is of enormous benefit to the other members of the class to be in close regular contact with Down's syndrome children.

AUTISM

General information

It is unlikely that teachers in a mainstream primary school will be asked to teach many autistic children during their careers. However, in some parts of the United Kingdom, autistic children are successfully integrated, both at primary and secondary levels. It is likely that teachers will hear and read about autism and maybe hear of children being described as having autistic tendencies or exhibiting autistic-type behaviour. Therefore it is worth looking at this condition, particularly in terms of educational issues. It was only in 1943 that autistic children were distinguished from other groups of children with forms of mental handicap, brain damage or sensory impairment; Kanner (1943) wrote a paper describing the particular characteristics which seemed to separate this particular group of children from others. Similar lists of features have been proposed subsequently by many other commentators. Autistic children are an extensively written about group of children! The lists of common features usually include the following items (this list was suggested by Lask and Lask, 1981);

- onset before the age of 2½ years;
- severe difficulties in socialization;

- severe difficulties and delay in understanding and using language;
- obsessional insistence on sameness, i.e. a reluctance to accept change in routines or the physical organization of the child's environment;
- gaze avoidance;
- lack of symbolic play.

Some autistic children may also exhibit:

- repetitive and ritualistic movements;
- a short attention span;
- self-injury.

The incidence of autism is approximately 1 in 2500 and it affects boys more than girls in a ratio of 2 or 3 to 1. The causes are unknown, although a variety of theories have been proposed. Rutter (1974) concluded that autism appears to be due to an inborn cognitive deficit involving the inability to acquire an inner language. This inner language, in most children, helps them to make sense of their experiences and to relate to people in a social sense. If this facility or capacity is not present, then it makes remedying the situation almost impossible, as we shall see.

Issues of integration

There is still no agreement among professionals about the nature of autism and whether it is, in fact, a single identifiable condition. The way the diagnosis is made in terms of the criteria used, the length of time taken and the interpretation of findings can make a difference in terms of the setting in which the child is placed and the type of education or treatment he receives. It is unfortunate if a premature or incorrect diagnosis is made, for then the autism 'label' can adversely affect expectations of what the child can achieve.

Teaching implications

The education of autistic children has received a great deal of attention but there are no firm conclusions about which teaching methods are most effective. Certainly, the curriculum which is offered to autistic children needs to be very wide as the ability range is great. Structured, behavioural approaches work well with some children with some tasks, but the overriding problem is one of generalization: often, skills can be taught in one context, but because of the importance of continuity and 'sameness' to autistic children and their dislike of change, they find it very hard to use the newly acquired skills in other settings. Some useful progress is made with some children by using approaches centred around music, games and dance. However, the qualities of the teacher and assistants seem to be central. They need to demonstrate flexibility, empathy and enormous patience.

The behaviour of autistic children can be quite bizarre and, in some cases, dangerous. It is therefore quite difficult for them to integrate into settings with large groups of children. Also, they often find social relations difficult and often do not appear to enjoy or understand the company of others. It is therefore questionable whether any large-scale integration is of benefit to an autistic child, as there are better ways of improving their skills of social interaction. Occasionally, integration does work but this is more often with very bright autistic children. Some of the latter seem to form a sub-group, who have what is known as Asberger's syndrome. These children may have very highly developed skills in certain areas, e.g. memory, computational skills, art, music, but very mediocre skills in other areas. The incidence of this condition in children is rare.

SPEECH AND LANGUAGE DIFFICULTIES

General information

Speech and language problems can occur as a result of some overall condition or impairment, as we have seen in earlier sections of this chapter. They can also occur in isolation and very often their cause is unknown. It is a complex area of study, with a variety of specific problems which can hinder children's development. In order to simplify things, it is useful to consider two categories of problem: *delayed speech and language* and *disordered speech and language*.

Delayed speech and language follow the normal developmental pattern but involve the late appearance of words and their combination into phrases and sentences. The child's speech is less mature than that of his peers, resembling the speech of a much younger child. The delay might be overall or it could affect one area more than others. It can be the sounds the child uses (*phonology*) which are immature, or the child's sentence structure (*syntax*) or possibly the way in which he is able to use language. In other cases, it may be the child's *comprehension* of spoken language that is affected. This is often termed *receptive language*.

Disordered speech and language is more complex, as progress does not follow the normal developmental sequence, in terms of the time of onset, rate of progress and patterns of acquisition. *Dysphasia*, in its receptive form, is an impaired ability to understand the rules

111

governing the language heard or to grasp its meaning. Expressive dysphasia is an inability to formulate language appropriately. In the latter case the comprehension of language may be unimpaired.

Another term which is used to describe particular problems is *dyspraxia*. This can be defined as the inability to imitate and reproduce correctly the muscular movements of the tongue and mouth necessary to make speech sounds. This is not due to any physical difficulty or paralysis but is characterized by poor articulation and indistinct speech sounds.

Language is an important skill, as it reflects, facilitates and mediates intellectual and social growth. Children with such difficulties will be disadvantaged in a variety of aspects of their education. It is therefore important that they are identified as early as possible, given a thorough assessment and then are able to have access to the correct support, teaching and therapy.

Issues of integration

Speech and language problems can vary enormously in their degree of severity and therefore in the effect they have on the child's life. Many children with minor speech problems, such as a lisp, a mild stammer or some immature language constructions, go through their school career in mainstream classes with no attention to their problem and no major setbacks resulting from it. Other children's speech may cause concern to parents or teachers and result in referral to a speech therapist. In most areas speech therapists are employed by health authorities and work from local clinics or health centres. They tend to see children individually or in small groups to try to remediate their difficulties. Therapists provide advice to parents on appropriate activities, games and approaches to help with their child's particular problem. Some therapists go into schools and will give advice and programmes of work to teachers either as an alternative form of service delivery or to complement the therapy they are undertaking with a child.

Children with more severe problems may need higher levels of specialized teaching and therapy and therefore they may be placed in separate settings. There are some special schools for children with speech and language problems but, in recent years, units attached to mainstream schools have been preferred. This is mainly because one of the crucial factors in improving children's language skills is the presence of plenty of normal language in the child's environment. Therefore, attempts are made to include the child in mainstream classes for subjects such as PE, Craft and others and also to ensure they take part in regular school events like assembly, playtime, dinnertime and outings. While in a special school or unit, the child will be in regular contact with a speech therapist and a specialist teacher. Structured language programmes are devised for each individual as a way of remediating his problems and accelerating his rate of progress. Many children return to mainstream schools after a period of specialist help but, for a few, specialist support will always be needed throughout their school careers.

Teaching implications

The identification of speech and language difficulties can be easy when children have obvious speech difficulties. However, a child with a complex receptive disorder may not be identified for years as this problem may have been assumed to be a part of a wider problem. Class teachers with a child suffering from such a disorder in their class will need support and guidance. This support may come from a speech therapist, a specialist visiting teacher or an educational psychologist.

In terms of a teaching approach for children with speech and language difficulties, it is useful to refer to the principles which can be gleaned from normal language learning in order to build up programmes of work. These may include:

- the need to select in advance and to be very specific about the particular words and constructions to be taught;
- the need to teach these items in a developmental order, as far as this is possible;
- the need to ensure that the language used by the teacher and other adults is simplified so that it relates to the child's development levels, existing vocabulary and comprehension;
- the need to build in plenty of repetition, both in terms of instruction and also response from the child, to ensure that learning has occurred;
- the need to check regularly to ensure that the child has retained what has been taught earlier;
- the need to establish and to adhere to a precise policy for the correction of errors, which should be followed by all staff;
- the need to present the same construction in a variety of situations in order to aid the generalization of the skill learnt.

It is sometimes the case that children with speech and language problems develop associated problems. This is predictable since the learning environment of the child will be affected in many ways by communication difficulties. The situation is not helped by the high level of verbal interaction between the teacher and the child and the child and his peers, which is a crucial part of school life. Some of these children experience difficulties in learning to read, spell and write and some have problems in sequencing. Sequencing problems can range from finding it difficult to dress (i.e. put clothes on in the right order) to finding difficulty in learning the days of the week or telling the time.

There may also be associated social or emotional problems. The child may become understandably frustrated by his inability to communicate and this may cause him to withdraw or to become aggressive. He may also experience difficulty in forming or maintaining friendships with his classmates.

CHAPTER SUMMARY

In considering some groups of children with a variety of special needs, this chapter has attempted to demystify certain conditions, to provide basic information and to give practical suggestions and advice on the needs of children who are likely to be encountered by primary teachers. It is hoped that special schools and special children will not be perceived by teachers as being so very different once they have read this chapter and had the opportunity to follow up some of the points raised.

SUGGESTIONS FOR FURTHER READING

Aarons, M. and Gittens, T. (1992) *Handbook of Autism*. London: Routledge. A very comprehensive and informative introduction to the subject.

Bleck, E. E. and Nagel, D. A. (1975) *Physically Handicapped Children: A Medical Atlas for Teachers*. New York: Grune & Stratton. A detailed reference book, which should be available in every school.

Dawkins, J. (1991) *Models of Mainstreaming for Visually Impaired Pupils*. London: HMSO. A more specialized text for those who are interested. It includes information on provision, some case studies and some useful appendices containing basic information.

Furneaux, B. and Roberts, B. (1977) *Autistic Children: Teaching, Community and Research Approaches*. London: Routledge & Kegan Paul. This is a balanced book which discusses autism and its treatment from a variety of angles.

Gregory, R.L. (1966) *Eye and Brain: The Psychology of Seeing*. London: Weidenfeld & Nicolson. A fascinating book for anyone wishing to know more about how the eye works and how this relates to the functioning of the brain.

Howarth, S.B. (1987) *Effective Integration: Physically Handicapped Children in Primary Schools*. Windsor: NFER-Nelson. A look at practical problems and solutions surrounding the integration of children with physical difficulties.

Locke, A. (1985) *Living Language*. Windsor: NFER-Nelson. A package of materials, in three stages, which can be used to develop language skills in young and developmentally delayed children. It includes plenty of ideas and resources for classroom teachers.

Male, J. and Thompson, C. (1985) *The Educational Implications of Disability: A Guide for Teachers*. London: Royal Association for Disability and Rehabilitation. A text which considers the topics addressed in this chapter in more depth and detail.

Solity, J. and Bickler, G. (eds) (1993) *Support Services*. London: Cassell. A valuable overview of the work and roles of the various support services that may become involved in dealing with the groups of children discussed in their chapter.

Webster, A. and Ellwood, J. (1985) *The Hearing Impaired Child in the Ordinary School*. Beckenham: Croom Helm. An authoritative book covering, as its title suggests, all aspects involved in the mainstreaming of children with hearing difficulties.

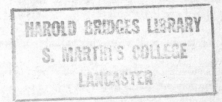

CHAPTER 8

Early identification and interventions with pre-school children

CHAPTER OVERVIEW

The purpose of this chapter is to fill a knowledge gap about what happens to pre-school children with special needs and to offer teachers a broad overview of the range of possible support mechanisms for parents and children. One particular form of support, known as the Portage system, is of particular interest to teachers and we will argue that this model contains many aspects of the most helpful forms of child and parent support as well as offering valuable information to the receiving school.

The involvement of parents in all aspects of pre-school education is vitally important, particularly in regard to the process of assessment and subsequent decision making about special needs pupils. We will describe examples of good practice in this regard as well as highlighting the importance of good playgroups, pre-school activities and nursery experience.

THE NEED TO KNOW ABOUT THE PRE-SCHOOL FIELD

When teachers welcome pupils into reception classes, a significant part of the pupils' lives has already taken place. For children with special needs, this is particularly the case; parents may view the start of their child's formal education as the culmination of a significant amount of work and effort by themselves and other professionals. For entirely understandable reasons, teachers are often unaware of what the child and the parents have been through, how many other professionals have already been involved and the procedures that have been enacted.

Some children will not arrive at their local primary school as they will have been placed in some form of special education. We believe that teachers need to know about the background and range of processes involved in such cases as well as appreciating the importance that must be attached to any Statements of Special Educational Need held by pupils entering reception classes.

IDENTIFYING CHILDREN WITH SPECIAL NEEDS AT THE PRE-SCHOOL STAGE

Broadly speaking, there are two main groups of children: those whose medical conditions can be identified at, or shortly following, birth and those whose needs are identified in their early years. The complexity of many conditions makes it impossible to provide hard and fast rules as there will always be exceptions. More important, it is necessary to recognize that individual variations are evident within all conditions. It is unwise to hold expectations about special needs pupils on the basis of the label applied to their condition.

CONDITIONS RECOGNIZABLE AT BIRTH

A good deal of our work as educational psychologists involves the pre-school field and brings us into contact with parents who have experienced being told that their newborn baby has a particular handicapping condition, such as Down's syndrome, spina bifida, severe brain damage, a physically disabling condition and a wide range of other conditions, some of which are genetically determined.

Breaking such news is, obviously, a harrowing experience for the medical staff concerned as well as a potentially devastating blow for the parents. How this difficult and delicate task has been handled can have a long-standing impact on how the parents react and cope with subsequent situations.

Breaking the news to parents

Understandably, this whole area of practice is an emotional issue and one which can cause acute upset and anxiety for parents even several years after the event. Thankfully, there is growing evidence that hospital staff, in particular doctors, usually prompted by feedback from parents, have considerably improved their handling of such situations. It must be recognized, however, that this is not true in all cases. Some parents are able to recount the most distressing and harrowing accounts of how the news was broken to them.

More and more hospitals appear to be establishing specific policies determining how the news should be broken to parents, in what situations, with specific follow-up support and giving those most essential qualities of time and patience. It is a prerequisite, however, that all staff concerned need to be trained in the skills necessary for this onerous task. In particular, staff should seek feedback and advice from parents who have been through the experience.

Coping with the news: the early stages

Much has been written about the processes which parents and the wider family groups go through during the early years of a special child's life. Many practitioners in the field believe that parents have to *go through* a process which is similar to that following the death of a loved one. They contend that, in a sense, parents have to grieve for the perfectly healthy child they expected but lost before they can begin to come to terms with, and even to love, the child who has been born to them. Many parents express feelings of guilt, anger and often great emotional pain, sometimes bordering on despair, as the sheer stress of their lives begins to impact.

This is not to say that parents and families always follow standard patterns of reaction. Goodey (1991) carried out in-depth interviews with nearly 40 parents of children with Down's syndrome. He concluded (p. 170):

> Between the apparent extremes . . . lie all sorts of individual circumstances. Some parents' reaction to the diagnosis is nullified by the additional diagnosis of some form of life-threatening physical condition such as meningitis or a heart defect, which to them is more distressing. Some may have previously had a miscarriage or a child who has died. For others who went through distress, over and over again the *concrete* feelings behind the abstraction of 'shock' have to do, not with newly existing beings whom one doesn't know, but with existing people in one's life-partners, family, etc. And none of them fails to recognise where these negative feelings come from, that such feelings have been taught by a particular upbringing and environment.

It is important to recognize this and also to appreciate that there may well be cultural and religious factors which influence how people respond. Few parents want or need pity, particularly from teachers, who will often be viewed as part of a very positive approach to meeting their child's needs. The contention that special children have special parents possibly has some validity in the sense that they have to acquire different skills and inevitably may develop specific attitudes and a different outlook on education. Teachers may need to think through how they would feel, were they to be in a similar position; this may help them to be prepared to offer some of the extra support and help which such parents may require.

It may well be that the parents of a special needs child appear to be over-protective and, at times, more demanding, particularly when their child first starts school. It is not difficult to imagine why this might be the case nor to appreciate why parents may still not have come to terms with the emotions and demands that have been placed on them at the time of their child's birth.

Across the UK there is considerable variation in what support is offered to the parents and when or how it is offered. After they have received the news, usually from a consultant paediatrician, a range of different professionals attempt to offer their support and help. There is always a variation in which services are available, but they often include specialist counsellors and staff who can offer advice and help of a practical kind. One of the most consistently valued inputs is not that of a professional but of a parent who has an older child with the same condition. Parent-to-parent discussions can be more personal and can address the really important issues in a less threatening way. Inter-parent support can be a valuable part of the whole process of assisting new parents to cope with the demands of their child with special needs.

Depending on the particular needs of the child, a variety of professionals can become involved with the family. This amount of input can, in itself, become a burden to parents, who might find themselves faced with a bewildering array of new people in their lives. Some children have a number of consultants involved in their treatment, such as a paediatrician, a neurologist, an orthopaedic specialist, a cardiac specialist and so on. In addition there are the paramedical staff, such as physiotherapists, occupational therapists, speech therapists, health visitors and community nurses.

Each has a different role to perform but obviously they cannot all operate in splendid isolation from each other. The Children Act 1989, which is having a major impact on the way in which children are dealt with by all involved, calls upon such agencies to act collaboratively in supporting children in need and their families. The requirement for this collaboration is particularly vital at the pre-school level. Co-ordinated input can, however, be completely disastrous if the key decision-makers, i.e. the parents, are not volved. Strange and horrifying as it may now seem, in the past parents were excluded from planning meetings about their children. Regrettably, there are still practitioners who believe that they know what is best for the family and can therefore make decisions on behalf of parents. Well-intentioned though they may be, it is extremely arrogant not to involve parents in all possible decisions and to prepare them in this way to assume responsibility for deciding what they want and what their child needs. Difficulties in communication with parents for whom English is a second language can be overcome by the use of interpreters, the translation of written materials and the use of video- and audio-tapes to aid recollection.

CONDITIONS IDENTIFIED DURING THE EARLY YEARS

The group of children for whom this applies is enormously diverse, sharing only the factor that the children's needs were not recognized at birth. It could include children who are eventually identified as presenting any of the following:

- developmental delay;
- sensory disabilities;
- cerebral palsy;
- a broad range of physical disabilities;
- speech and language delays and disorders;
- learning problems;
- a combination of the above.

How are these children identified?

There is no simple answer to this question, although there are key people to whom parents will turn when they have worries about their child. It is often the case, not surprisingly, that first-time parents or those who are separated from the advice and support of their own families take longer to recognize their child's problems.

Parents often turn in the first instance to their health visitor or to their general practitioner (GP) to seek advice on whether their concerns have any validity or require further investigations. Their GP might well refer them to an appropriate consultant, or consultants, and this should be the beginning of collaborative work between parents and professionals.

Sometimes, because of the less obvious impact of some of these conditions, a concern can be first noted at a baby screening session. These are usually conducted in community settings by health visitors, school medical officers and, increasingly, by family doctors.

In this case it is the professional registering the initial concern and bringing it to the attention of the parent. How this is handled can have a critical impact on how parents cope with the ensuing demands.

In ideal circumstances, it should mark the start of a period of assessment. All too often, however, parents are told what the long-term implications *will* be, rather than being given an indication of various possible outcomes. At this stage, of course, parents are understandably anxious to be given definite information on the longer-term implications, yet much damage can be inflicted by professionals who feel, for whatever reasons, that they can predict the outcome of the assessment. Given the individual variations and the fact that the assessment will need to be multi-professional, such pronouncements are rash. They give parents definite expectations, which is antithetical to the whole purpose and process of the assessment period.

What happens after the initial identification?

The next stages involve determining the nature of the child's problems in detail, assessing the child's needs, and deciding what support will be necessary. There is an enormous regional variation in how, where and when these stages are enacted. The geographical setting, rural or urban, can have a real bearing on the availability of specialist resources and the capacity of the family to travel to such facilities. Local health authorities have determined their own policies in regard to the siting of Child Development or Assessment Centres. A great deal seems to depend on whether key consultants, particularly paediatricians, see their role as community- or hospital-based. Encouragingly, it is becoming recognized that to be really effective and helpful to parents, the specialist help needs to be moved out into the community and even into homes.

As soon as a problem or concern is identified, the parents need more than just a diagnosis or assessment; they require support that is practical and emotionally helpful, but which is also geared to their actual needs. Again, there cannot be a common or simple formula to fit all situations.

The assessment process cannot, nor should it, be separated out from the ongoing provision of support and help to the child and the parents. In pragmatic terms, parents cannot wait for the full diagnosis when they are experiencing very real difficulties with their child's feeding or sleeping patterns.

Generally speaking, there will be a number of aspects to the initial assessment of the child, each of which may well be incorporated into the formal process of assessment under the 1981 Education Act. The key elements are as follows.

Medical investigations

Consultants and their medical colleagues will attempt to define the precise nature of the child's condition. Thus, for example, it will be necessary to identify whether the child has a cardiac problem, a sensory difficulty, an orthopaedic difficulty, a neurological problem, and so on. In this process the expertise of paramedical staff including physiotherapists, occupational therapists and speech therapists, could be called upon. Involving such an array of people, however necessary, brings with it inherent difficulties: the child will need to be seen by and examined by each of these professionals, often over an extended period of time, entailing a plethora of appointments at hospitals and clinics.

Educational investigations

To speak of educational investigations is a loose way of describing the early stages of defining a child's developmental and educational needs and teaching targets, which may involve specialist teachers, nursery nurses, psychologists and/or play workers. Inevitably, there is an overlap between educational and medical assessment. Indeed, such overlap is the essence of a multi-disciplinary approach to assessment and support. The two types of assessment should inform and facilitate the *overall* assessment of the child.

Where does the process of assessment take place?

For parents this is a logistically and psychologically significant matter. The concept of child development centres attached to hospitals arose from the need to streamline the assessment process for parents by bringing all the professionals together under one roof, where they can be on hand at once to offer advice and help to parents and to each other. There are many examples of good practice. Centres have become resource bases for parents, as well as assessment centres; in certain cases, parents have become involved in the management of the projects.

While it is obviously necessary to conduct assessments requiring technological equipment in hospitals, it is questionable whether all the other aspects of the assessment need to be conducted in such an inevitably clinical environment. No matter how hard staff try to ensure that the child development centre looks and feels different from the rest of the hospital, the fact remains that many parents feel uncomfortable linking the assessment of their child with an institution for people who are seriously ill.

To some extent, the problem has been successfully overcome by siting child development centres away from hospitals out in the community, often attached to or based in health centres. Nevertheless, there still remains the more pervasive problem of which is the best setting in which to assess a very young child to ensure that the truest possible picture of the youngster's skills and difficulties is achieved. Overall, children usually perform most successfully in a familiar environment and working with their parents. Thus the child's home is the place in which he is likely to perform most successfully. It is also the environment in which the parents will feel most comfortable and confident. There is therefore a dilemma over where the process of assessment should be conducted. Encouragingly, such work is increasingly being conducted in the home by teachers, psychologists and doctors.

Models of assessment

The model of assessment used by professionals is a crucially important issue. On the one hand there is the *medical*, on the other, the *assessment-over-time* model. The disagreement between adherents of the two models parallels the one over the assessment of pupils in the classroom.

The *medical model* could be represented as the view that a child can either perform a task or not (in much the same way as a patient either has or does not have a medical condition) and that the situation in which the testing is carried out is largely irrelevant. Additionally, the medical model conceives of assessment as a route to *diagnosis*, which will largely be concerned with factors assumed to be *within the child*, such as intelligence or ability.

The assessment-over-time approach is based on the argument that a child's skills are best assessed over a period, in response to direct teaching and in an environment in which the child feels most comfortable, usually the home.

The argument is more than just a disagreement between differing professional groups; it has an impact on how the parents feel about the assessment outcomes. If parents feel that they have been involved in the process, that they have been consulted at all possible stages and that they have been able to participate actively, then they are more likely to accept and to agree with the outcomes. If, however, the assessment has been conducted away from them in an alien environment they feel little sense of ownership in the outcomes.

It would seem that the latter scenario now occurs less often.

Despite the organizational difficulties involved in a thorough and comprehensive assessment of a child over time, the general trend would seem to be away from a total adherence to the medical model. The need to involve parents more directly in the assessment of their pre-school child is being increasingly acknowledged.

Formal assessments under the 1981 Education Act

After the process of identification, it may be decided to recommend to the parents a *formal* assessment of their child's needs, under the terms of the 1981 Education Act (see Chapter 9, pp. 137–40). The exact procedures and legal requirements relating to under-fives are complex and there is considerable variation between different education and health authorities. It is worth noting, however, that health authorities have a legal responsibility to inform the LEA of children under five who *might* have special educational needs.

As a general rule, it is usually in a child's best interests to begin the process of formal assessment in his third year. Thus for children with severe learning difficulties, whose needs cannot be met in even pre-school mainstream provision, it will be possible to complete the process through to a formal statement and to secure placement in specialist provision. Correspondingly, a proportion of children are, with their parents' approval, placed in a special school or specialist integrated nurseries from three years of age.

Under the terms of the 1981 Education Act, a child of under two years of age can be formally assessed, exactly how being a matter determined by the LEA. In practice this option is rarely used. There are only a few circumstances, such as a child with a particularly complex medical condition, when a placement in a special school is necessary before a child's second birthday.

For pre-school children with less serious learning difficulties the process of formal assessment may lead, depending on the LEA's policy, to their being issued with a statement, and the resultant specific resources to enable them to take up a place in ordinary nursery classes.

For children with severe learning difficulties, the process of *formal* assessment will have been completed with the issuing of a statement and placement. Although the child's needs must be reviewed on an annual basis, their immediate needs will have been defined at this pre-school stage. For children whose needs are not clearly defined by this stage and, indeed, whose needs may become more clearly defined only as they participate in nursery or pre-school activity, no such protection exists.

From the foregoing it can be seen, first, that the pre-school phase is of crucial importance, particularly when the process of formal assessment is conducted while the child is attending a nursery class, second, that there is no golden rule with regard to how and when pre-school children's needs are assessed and where their needs should be met. It is possible that, upon completion of the formal assessment, a placement at a special school or unit will be considered the most appropriate way of meeting the child's needs. Other children may be issued with statements indicating placements in mainstream settings.

WHAT SUPPORT DO PARENTS NEED DURING THE PRE-SCHOOL YEARS?

There is a danger, in trying to offer an answer to such an important question, of making assumptions about *all* parents in this position, without recognizing the need to treat people as distinct individuals. Much of the early literature in this field is riddled with well-intentioned but fundamentally flawed advice on what 'they' need at certain stages. Earlier on in the chapter we referred to the array of different professionals who can become involved; we also referred to the benefits which *some* parents draw from talking to other parents who have been in a similar position to themselves. Just as the needs of individual children differ, so too do those of their parents.

The onus is on statutory bodies to ensure that their services are co-ordinated effectively and that parents and care-givers are offered appropriate access to their resources. Parental choice should be a key factor. Thus parents should be able to elect to receive a particular service or not, to join a particular group or not, and should be able to influence if, how and where the assessment of their child is conducted. In addition, real choice means that the parents should have the right to opt into and out of a service at a later stage, rather than its being offered on a once-and-for-all basis.

In a bid to improve the co-ordination of such inputs to parents, many locally based service providers have joined together to ensure a greater degree of communication and efficiency. Such an arrangement would include staff from the local Health Service, the Social Services Department and the Education Department. Increasingly, voluntary organizations are becoming involved, offering a variety of services, often in partnership with local authorities. Ideally, parents who are offered choice should have the opportunity to find out in some detail what is being offered before making a decision. It is therefore incumbent upon all such services to ensure that they operate in an efficient and organized manner.

The following are some of the services offered to parents by statutory and voluntary agencies.

Specialist teachers

Peripatetic specialist teachers are usually experts in fields such as sensory impairments (both vision and hearing), mental handicap, physical disabilities or language difficulties. They offer specific practical advice and also access to the resources of their employing authority. They can give parents informed advice on the special and mainstream schools in their area, as well as detailed guidance on what will be taught to their child in the early stages of the National Curriculum. Advice can therefore be given on what the schools will need to do by way of adapting their teaching materials, teaching style and learning environment in order to ensure that the child has the fullest possible access to the National Curriculum.

Specialist social workers

Specialist social workers have expert knowledge of the legislation relating to parents' rights, and the benefits for which they can claim. Many are also counsellors, with the expertise to help parents cope with the various emotional, personal, marital and practical difficulties that might arise.

Information systems and resource bases

Information systems and resource bases are designed to enable parents and professionals to find out what is available both locally and nationally by way of support and advice. Many such organizations are small, having been set up on a self-help basis, possibly geared to a specific and rare condition. Through these databases and networks parents can often discover facilities to which they are entitled, such as specialist babysitting services, grant-making charities, holidays, specialist playschemes, toy libraries, shared-care facilities, respite care arrangements, etc.

Voluntary groups and national organizations

Parents often report feeling totally isolated once they have accepted that their child has a particular difficulty or condition. This is the point at which talking to a parent who has been in a similar position can be extremely helpful. In our experience, many long-lasting and mutually supportive relationships have developed in this way.

Parents may find it beneficial to join a national organization that will provide information about their child's condition, research, contact networks and fund-raising activities. Just as important, many such organizations provide social activities for the whole family and opportunities to chat in a relaxed atmosphere. Many see it as part of their role to inform and to support professionals working with their children. Such a starting-point can prove to be enormously valuable to a teacher seeking to learn about a particular condition.

One particular approach to supporting parents in their homes is worthy of particular notice not only because of its well-established reputation for meeting parents and children's needs, but also because of the many valuable implications its work has for teachers. This is the Portage system.

THE PORTAGE SYSTEM

Historical background and current status

The Portage approach is named after a town in Wisconsin, where the original model was developed as a way of providing support to families in a largely rural community whose children had special needs. It was introduced into the United Kingdom in the early 1970s as an answer to the problem of providing parents of pre-school special needs children with practical advice and training in how they could best teach their children. The approach carried with it the benefits of providing the service in the family home and ensuring a high degree of parental involvement in all aspects of work.

The model and its many adaptations and expansions have been rigorously evaluated and have compared well to other forms of pre-school interventions. The conclusions indicate that when systematically organized and monitored, the Portage approach enables children to make significant developmental gains as well as providing a much broader form of support to parents (see, for example, Cameron, 1982).

Currently, there are approximately 140 services throughout the United Kingdom and a thriving National Portage Association. There are Portage services in India, Japan, Italy, Romania and many other countries. The views of parents expressed at National Portage Conferences give an indication of the sizeable contribution of Portage services in the United Kingdom. Obviously there is a danger that such an approach in a highly sensitive and emotional area can develop a charismatic or evangelical orientation, taking its operations beyond the reach of objective enquiry. However, the model does have in-built systems for self-monitoring and for ensuring high levels of quality service delivery.

What is Portage?

Portage is essentially a prescribed system of supporting parents in their own homes. While the model is flexible and open to useful adaptations, there are certain essential aspects which provide quality and professional rigour for which Portage has a justifiable reputation. A Portage service will be based on a number of key personnel:

Portage advisers, who visit families on a regular weekly basis to work with the parents teaching them how to teach specific skills to their children. Advisers come from a variety of backgrounds and include teachers, health visitors, speech therapists, community nurses, social workers, nursery nurses and child care workers. Encouragingly, many are now volunteers with no formal qualifications and, most valuably, former service recipients. All need to have been trained on a specific course approved by the National Portage Association and must be appropriately supervised. Many experienced advisers are moving on to become supervisors.

Portage supervisors tend to be members of a particular professional group which has a background of expertise in this type of work, such as psychologists or specialist health workers. Most will have worked as advisers themselves. Supervisors are charged with the responsibility of ensuring high standards of service delivery by observing the working practice of the advisers and by checking on the weekly progress of all participating children through direct feedback and record-keeping. In turn, the supervisors are accountable to a Portage management committee.

The management committee is the overseeing group to which all service providers are responsible. Initially, such groups tended to be composed of senior representatives of the various bodies who funded, either directly or indirectly, the service. The original brief of ensuring that the investment of their organization was well managed tended to subside as the newly established service established its levels of quality. Most management groups have found themselves dealing with issues relating to the needs of individual parents, the practice of the advisers, the development of the project and fund-raising. Once again, parents have tended to become actively involved in these groups, ensuring that the direction of the services has suited their needs rather than those of the contributing bodies.

Portage in practice: what teachers can learn from the approach

Once a family has referred itself to the service, an adviser will visit to explain the commitments on both sides and then to begin the process of finding out what the child can and cannot do already. (In many ways, this is a situation analogous to that in which teachers find themselves when initially introduced to a special needs child.) The Portage adviser then completes a checklist. It is important to recognize that the parents' involvement at every stage is crucial, but particularly at this the assessment phase.

The checklist is like many similar tools in that it is a list of precise skills which are in a general developmental sequence. Parents are asked a series of discrete questions as to whether their child has developed a particular skill or not. The skills are grouped together under broad headings such as Early Infant Stimulation, Language, Motor Skills, Cognitive Skills, and so on, and are listed, within the groupings, in a general developmental sequence.

Some caution is called for, however. The sequence should not be seen by those involved as definitive or an indication of how *normal children* develop. At best, such a sequence is a broad-brush approach to the general order in which children's skills and stages of development tend to emerge. The Portage checklist includes a general indication of the age in months at which groups of skills tend to emerge or to develop. Again, caution needs to be used in the interpretation of these *age equivalents* as children vary enormously in their individual patterns of development.

In the analogous classroom situation, teachers may use a checklist, related to their curriculum structure, against which they can check the child's progress and thereby assess the child's skill levels. As with the Portage method, it is valuable to enlist the parents in this process, particularly in the case of very young pupils. If the parent is unsure about a particular skill or if the child has never been given the opportunity to perform the task, the adviser will set up a mini-test using, wherever possible, the parent and familiar toys or materials from the home. This completion of the checklist and any other related assessment tasks, such as analysing the child's language, can take several visits and is an important part of the whole procedure.

After completing the checklist, it is possible for the adviser and parent to analyse those areas in which the child may need specific help and where the teaching ought to be concentrated. In the classroom the teacher will also be in a position to analyse how the child's skills, as revealed by the completion of a checklist, measure up to the curriculum and to identify those areas for particular attention. In school the curricular demands will influence the specific programme of work on which the teacher will embark but at home other demands may have priority. Thus, the adviser will establish what the parent wants to work on; this dialogue is repeated at many future points and is a crucial part of ensuring that the parents feel that they are in real partnership with the adviser and the Portage service. The adviser who realizes which skills the child will *need* in order to tackle the school curriculum may well seek to influence the parents, but the parents' wishes must predominate wherever this is feasible and realistic. Parents will probably wish to concentrate initially on self-help areas, such as feeding and toileting, and areas which have an immediate impact on family life. Sometimes they may want to concentrate on eradicating a particular type of behaviour such as throwing, self-damage or screaming. A number of *long-term goals* are chosen and one selected on which to begin work.

The task for the adviser is to break that skill down into a sequence of small steps on which the parents and child can work gradually, leading to the achievement of the long-term goal. Here again is a teaching approach (known as *task analysis*) that can be used by teachers. The child is checked against this sequence to find the appropriate starting-point for the first week's activity.

The adviser has to demonstrate to the parents how best to teach the particular skill to their child. Various teaching techniques, originating in applied behavioural analysis and its applications to work with slow learners, form a large part of the advisers' initial training course. From her knowledge of these the adviser, with the help of the supervisor, will decide upon an appropriate technique. Many of these techniques will be familiar to teachers from their training (e.g. the use of prompting and gesture, imitational learning, chaining, the use of rewards and shaping). The adviser's aim will be to impart these skills and techniques to the parents over a period of time. Having demonstrated the technique with the precisely defined task, the adviser will encourage the parents to have a go. This needs to be done with an awareness of the parents' sensitivities and emotional involvement with the child, and demands considerable care and skill.

The key to the success of the Portage approach lies in its commitment to achieving successful outcomes for the parents and child. Thus, if the weekly activity is arranged correctly, the child should make progress towards the teaching goal. With this in view two important parts of the session include:

What to do when the child achieves success. In other words, how the child should be rewarded and with what. The emphasis throughout Portage is on teaching through positive reinforcement, minimizing errors and celebrating success.

What the parents should do if the child is failing on the task. The emphasis is upon introducing the minimum amount of additional help to enable the child to achieve this success. Such correctional techniques or prompts need to be used systematically and sensitively.

Once the parents feel comfortable with the week's activity, the adviser writes the agreement on an activity sheet detailing the main essentials:

- the skill which the child is being taught through the weekly activity;
- how the task or activity should be presented to the child, including what should be said;
- how to help the child if he starts to fail;
- how to reward the child *when* the task is achieved;
- how often to present the task to the child each day;
- how to chart the child's progress;
- the criterion of success for this activity.

There are many variations in the design and detail of activity charts, but the aim is always to achieve a detailed individual programme. It is an approach which could be carried into the classroom situation. The influence of behavioural objectives is evident in the design and detail of the whole process.

Portage relies on the parent carrying out the set activities regularly on the principle of 'a little and often', rather than extended, and possibly irregular, periods of teaching. This too is a practice that can be readily applied in the classroom. The parent charts the child's progress in detail but using a simple recording system of ticks and crosses. Such records enable advisers and parents on Portage to decide whether the child is making progress. A similar system in the classroom can enable the teacher to analyse the child's progress in detail and to assess the effectiveness of particular teaching strategies.

At the start of the following week's visit, the adviser will check on the child's record before asking the parent to demonstrate the progress achieved. This is then celebrated by all, because parents, as much as teachers and children, need to see progress and to receive rewards. Standing back and analysing the progress a child is achieving is important in terms of assessing whether teaching techniques need to be changed or the *size* of the task altered. Gradually, the parent and adviser develop a *feel* for the child in terms of how he learns best, what techniques seem to work, what are the most powerful rewards and what pace he seems to prefer. Inevitably, this will change as the child grows and it will vary with different activities. The participants, particularly the parents, seem to get better at predicting the best formula for particular activities.

This knowledge about the child clearly builds on, or grows out of, the very detailed understanding which most parents have about their children. Nevertheless, the extended use of the Portage system allows the parents to learn in some detail about how their child learns and, therefore, how best they can teach him. The situation in the class-room holds a good many parallels as the teacher gradually achieves a picture of, or a *feel* for, how the child learns best. It is essential, however, that this hard-won knowledge should not have to be learnt by each successive teacher. Good record-keeping and discussions should ensure that it is not lost.

Portage parents clearly can, if the intervention is successful, build up expertise which can be of advantage to the reception class teacher. Additionally, the process of using the Portage model provides much useful data for *assessment through teaching*. For children who have been in receipt of a Portage service or a similar system of regular weekly structured visits and direct teaching, the contribution that can be made to the formal process of assessment is significant.

Other aspects of the Portage system provide useful models for teachers. A relationship between the adviser and the parents (or one parent) usually becomes established as the Portage worker becomes an important part of the family's life. From a basis of offering essentially practical support often develops emotional and highly personal support. Such a relationship can develop between the parents of special needs children and their teacher. This is often one of the most rewarding and challenging aspects of such work.

The Portage model holds many similarities to successful classroom practice, the most crucial being the need to work in systematic short steps and, wherever practical, to involve parents in key decision-making. We would stress the benefits for teachers of spending time with a local Portage service to learn from its personnel's experience, skills and resources.

We have gone to some lengths to explain the Portage system in the belief that there are many useful aspects for the teacher. It must be stressed, however, that it is not the only successful approach to helping parents at this stage, nor is it universally available. A detailed overview of a range of alternative strategies and evaluation studies can be found in Cunningham and Glenn (1989). Equally, our account of Portage is not complete, for the model is being continually enhanced and developed.

SPECIAL NEEDS CHILDREN AND PRE-SCHOOL FACILITIES

Dessent (1987) argues strongly against isolating special needs children from their peers at this age level. There is an implicit danger, he contends, in allowing such children to become 'too special, too soon' (p. 98). Goacher *et al.* (1988), in reviewing the available provision for this age group, came to the conclusion that far too much of the provision for pupils with special needs was segregated (pp. 68 and 153). It is possible that the overall shortage of nursery schools has hampered the opportunities for special needs pupils to assume places in such provision.

The recently produced HMI report on nursery education (DES/HMI, 1989, p. 6, para. 9) provides further evidence of why this should be a problem:

> The quality of education for the under-fives in some LEAs suffers from a shortage of appropriately trained teachers and advisers with expertise covering this age of children. . . . Not surprisingly, such teachers find it difficult to provide and teach a suitable curriculum for young children. They need effective guidance and training to work with this age group.

In practice, there are nurseries attempting to offer an appropriate experience to special needs pupils. It is also the case that many children who have special educational needs are able to participate actively and profitably in playgroups and other organized pre-school activities because the nature of their particular difficulties may not yet impede their capacity to benefit from that which is ordinarily available. It may well be, for example, that with reasonably advanced motor development a child can benefit enormously from a placement in a nursery school, despite the fact that his language development is delayed. Additionally, most nurseries are single-storey buildings, not requiring much adaptation for children with physical disabilities. The Children Act has introduced a much broader definition of 'children in need', which should include the majority with special educational needs and should ensure this group greater access to whatever nursery education is available.

Receiving teachers of special needs children can, and should ensure that they do, benefit from the work of staff at nurseries, where the opportunities for structured play and early learning should have provided a great deal of valuable information about the child. This is particularly important for children with statements, as part of the very process of assessment on which the statement is based will probably have been conducted in the nursery. While free and structured play are essential aspects of a balanced nursery curriculum, direct skill teaching also has a central position and is all the more necessary for youngsters with special needs. Contact with the nursery staff and an exchange of records and information are therefore invaluable in the case of such pupils.

CHAPTER SUMMARY

The early years of a special needs child's life are particularly full and represent a number of crucial stages for parents. From early identification through the processes of assessment many demands will have been made of the child and his parents. It is essential that teachers should be aware of what has gone on in the pre-school years so that they can benefit from the outcomes and have an understanding of the experiences which parents have been through. It is often easier to appreciate parental attitudes and concerns against such background knowledge.

Practice in this area, though clearly shaped by legislation, varies considerably and the chapter sought to present several key issues to teachers. The Portage system of service delivery provides many useful models for teachers, particularly with regard to *assessment through teaching* and parental involvement. Mainstream teachers have much to gain from contact with practitioners in the pre-school field at a general level and certainly in regard to specific information and advice about particular children. The pre-school years lay the foundation for the child's education; this is more evidently the case for special needs pupils.

SUGGESTIONS FOR FURTHER READING

Cameron, R.J. (ed.) (1982) *Working Together: Portage in the UK*. Windsor: NFER-Nelson.

Cameron, R.J. (ed.) (1986) *Portage, Parents and Professionals: Helping Families with Special Needs*. Windsor: NFER-Nelson. Both of the above books are overviews of conferences organized by the National Portage Association. They have a practical orientation and will serve as a valuable introduction to the workings of the model.

Carr, J. (1980) *Helping Your Handicapped Child*. Harmondsworth: Penguin Books. Some of the terminology used in this book would be considered unacceptable nowadays. The ideas are sound, however, and coupled with lots of clearly written advice.

Cunningham, C. and Sloper, P. (1978). *Helping Your Handicapped Baby*. London: Souvenir Press. Very similar to the previous book, but with an emphasis on development in the first two years of life and a useful section on behaviour difficulties.

Daly, B., Addington, J., Kerfoot, S. and Sigston, A. (1985) *Portage: The Importance of Parents*. Windsor: NFER-Nelson. Another conference report but with the emphasis very much on the importance and roles of parents in partnership with professionals.

Kiernan, C., Jordan, R. and Saunders, C. (1978) *Starting Off*. London: Souvenir Press. A source of valuable ideas about behaviour management approaches, the development of teaching programmes and sensible guidance on communication and self-help skills.

McConkey, R. (1985) *Working with Parents: A Practical Guide for Teachers and Therapists*. Beckenham: Croom Helm. Teachers wishing to work in conjunction with parents and care-givers will find this a challenging and valuable source of advice and guidance. It is a book that can be dipped into and used as for reference purposes.

Pugh, G. and De'Ath, E. (1985) *The Needs of Parents*. Basingstoke: Macmillan. The authors examine in considerable detail many of the issues concerning parents which have been touched on in this chapter. There are some real 'pearls of wisdom' in this detailed book.

CHAPTER 9

Policies for special educational needs

CHAPTER OVERVIEW

We have seen how education policy can affect the lives of children with special needs; in this chapter we highlight key UK legislation which has altered and is still altering the way that schools are run and the way that children are dealt with. In particular, we consider the Education Act 1981, the Education Reform Act 1988 and the Children Act 1989. These Acts have had an impact on the rights of all children, but in some ways have affected special needs children more radically.

Although national legislation must be observed by all local authorities, there is often considerable scope for interpretation; thus some authorities will prioritize certain areas at the expense of others. So great is the variation between authorities in the implementation of the 1981 Education Act and the methods chosen to meet children's special needs that a survey of this area was undertaken jointly, at the government's request, by the Audit Commission and Her Majesty's Inspectorate (HMI). This report gives a picture of special needs policy and practice in local authorities throughout the United Kingdom and will help influence changes to existing, and help create future, legislation. In the light of the Commission's findings, our second section considers how decision-making at LEA level can affect special needs children.

Finally, the provision for and teaching of special needs children in individual schools varies dramatically. We propose a model for policy development which can be used in schools or can help individual teachers to decide how to tackle the special needs issues within their own class.

RECENT LEGISLATION

Background

The first major piece of education legislation this century was the Education Act 1944. Subsequent legislation, relating to children with special educational needs, either added to or replaced responsibilities invested in LEAs by this Act. During the 1970s the Warnock Committee researched practice in the area of special needs, and submitted its influential report, *Special Educational Needs* (DES, 1978), to Parliament in 1978.

The Education Act 1981

The 1981 Education Act introduced new definitions of *special educational needs*, *learning difficulties* and *special educational provision* (see pp. 23–6); parents' rights were established and their importance in the role of assessment and decision making was recognized. The importance of mainstream schooling for children, wherever possible, was emphasized (see Chapter 2).

Particularly significant for all teachers is the part of the 1981 Education Act that defines the statutory assessment procedure.

Assessment and statementing

It is very likely that in every school there are some children who either have a statement of their special educational needs, are being assessed to determine whether or not they should have a statement (or 'be statemented' in the more familiar, colloquial jargon), or being considered for statutory assessment. Terminology can become confused and confusing, particularly as locally based assessment procedures can exist alongside statutory arrangements.

The Warnock Report recommended that assessment of special educational needs should be a five-stage process, and although this is not a legal requirement, many local authorities have found the model a useful guide. The original concept was that the initial identification of the child (in a mainstream school) should be the responsibility of the headteacher and the staff. A second stage of assessment, and hopefully intervention, if the school is following an assessment-through-teaching model (see Chapter 4), might involve an advisory, specialist teacher coming in to support the child and the child's teachers. Next in the sequence would be an assessment by other outside professionals, for instance a speech therapist or an educational psychologist, after which there would be suggested a multi-professional assessment and, finally, a statutory assessment of the child's needs. In practice, this is an elaborate, indeed overcomplex, sequence but many authorities have condensed it to three stages of assessment, as shown below.

A three-stage model of assessment

(following guidelines given by the Warnock Report)

Stage 1 Involves the school assessing and working with a child or, in the case of pre-school children, the parents and initial caseworkers assessing and working with the child.

Stage 2 This is reached when the advice of visiting professionals is sought, in the case of schools, or referrals to other professionals are made in the case of pre-schoolers. Information gained at this stage, by implementing special programmes or enlisting extra support, should help to decide whether a statutory assessment of the child's needs is warranted.

Stage 3 If this stage is reached, the next step is to trigger the procedures to begin a statutory assessment under section 5 of the 1981 Education Act.

The process of statutory assessment is prescribed by section 5 of the 1981 Education Act, which is why the assessments are often referred to as *section 5 assessments*. The section requires LEAs to make an assessment of a child when they are of the opinion:

> that he has special educational needs which call for the authority to determine the special educational provision that should be made for him;

or

> that he probably has such needs. [subsection 1]

From this definition it can be seen that some form of preliminary assessment or some detailed, prior knowledge of the child must be available before the authority decides to initiate a statutory assessment.

Within local authorities it is usually an education officer (EO) or assistant education officer (AEO) within the Special Needs Section who acts on behalf of the authority to administer the process, but the request for a section 5 assessment may come from various sources within an LEA or directly from parents or health professionals.

When the LEA proposes to make an assessment it is obliged to:

* inform the child's parents of its intention;

- explain the procedure it will follow while making its assessment;
- give the name of an officer of the authority from whom further information may be obtained;
- invite the parents to submit their views on their child's difficulties, within a specified period of time.

If then the authority decides to proceed with an assessment it must inform the parents of the decision and seek *advice* from at least three, and sometimes more, professionals.

Who provides advice during a formal section 5 assessment?

Educational advice is always sought and must be provided by a qualified teacher who has taught the child within the past 18 months. In many cases, the educational advice is compiled on the basis of information from the class teacher, the headteacher and any other teachers who have had a sizeable amount of contact with the child. The type of information to be included in the educational advice is given in the accompanying circulars to the 1981 Act. The original circular was coded 1/83 (i.e. the first circular to be produced in 1983) but this has been replaced by 22/89, which was itself amended in 1992! The most useful advice will detail information about the child's recent educational progress, his strengths and weaknesses and the types of methods and approaches which work best with him. If an assessment-through-teaching approach has been used then a clear picture of the child's learning styles and his differential rates of progress can be provided.

Medical advice is also required and is usually provided by a doctor working for the school health service or, for pre-school children, a paediatrician. It is based on the child's medical records and a recently conducted medical examination. Any recommendations should relate to the child's *educational* needs rather than to his general medical needs. Thus the advice should detail any difficulties the child might have, very often sensory or physical, and explain the *implications* of these problems in terms of the child's education. The medical advice includes information provided by other medical and paramedical staff, including consultants, speech therapists and physiotherapists.

Psychological advice, the final statutory type of advice that is required, must be provided by a qualified educational psychologist employed by the local authority. The psychologist has usually been involved with the child prior to the formal assessment and has, in many cases, been working with teachers to plan programmes or to change behaviours. The psychologist's advice should consider all the child's difficulties before determining his various needs (at home and at school) and recommending ways of meeting them.

In addition to these three pieces of advice, the LEA can seek advice from other professionals such as voluntary agencies, social workers or Portage advisers.

After the authority has considered all this advice, copies of the documents are sent to the parents, accompanied by a *draft* or *proposed statement* of the child's special educational needs, in cases where the authority has decided that a statement is appropriate. When one is not considered appropriate, the parents are advised of this and informed of their rights of appeal. The draft statement will detail the child's needs and list the provision the authority intends to make to meet them, which may consist of placement in a special school or unit, or the providing of extra support and resources in a mainstream school. The child's parents are given a specified period of time to consider the proposed statement, question the advice and possibly to visit schools, if they have not already done so. Once any issues have been resolved, the authority will then issue a *final statement*, which is a legally binding document.

Statements must be reviewed annually, which is the responsibility of the child's headteacher, and at the age of 13½ each 'statemented' child is entitled to a full reassessment of his needs. This is to ensure that appropriate early planning is undertaken to cater for each child during his last two years of school and also at post-16 level. It is important that Social Services or voluntary agencies are informed of children with severe or complex problems so they can provide the necessary community support, day centres or respite care. Indeed, this is where the 1981 Education Act can link with the requirements of the Disabled Persons Act.

Statemented children in mainstream schools

Chapter 7 considered children with specific types of handicap and discussed the range of support which would be needed for them to benefit from mainstream education. Most children who are provided with support or resources which are *over and above that which is normally available* will have a statement which lists the support to be provided and should usually be a guarantee to the child and parents that the provision will be maintained.

Local authorities vary in their statementing policy. At one extreme, some authorities require a statement to be issued before any external support, such as peripatetic, specialist teachers or learning support, can be provided for an individual child. At the other extreme, some authorities view all their support services as being *normally available* to all children who need them. In these authorities statements would only be issued for children in mainstream schools when something unusual was required, such as placement in a special school or unit.

The Audit Commission Report (1992) noted that authorities also vary greatly in the amount of detail and specificity required in statements. Overall, the Commission concluded that statements tended to be woolly and generalist with the result that 'contrary to the intention of the 1981 Act, they cannot guarantee a specific level of provision' (p. 1). Some authorities admitted that statements were deliberately written in vague terms because the high cost of provision discourages them from making open-ended financial commitments. At a time when LEAs are having to control their budgets tightly, decisions are not always made with the best interests of the children at heart, but rather on financial grounds. The process of assessing a child under section 5 of the 1981 Act is very costly. A statement can commit the authority to providing expensive resources over several years. Therefore some authorities have changed their criteria for statementing since the Act came into force ten years ago.

Whether or not to statement?

Attitudes towards statements have also changed over this time. At first, to have the so-called 'protection' of a statement was seen as being a good thing: it defined needs precisely, guaranteed appropriate, well-resourced provision, and should have enabled more access to mainstream schools. However, the Act was introduced with no extra money from central government and authorities were forced to look to their own resources in order to fund these more costly assessments and the extra costs of supporting children in mainstream settings.

The Warnock Report had envisaged fewer children being educated in segregated special provision as more attended mainstream schools, with an accompanying transfer of funds from special to mainstream education. This has not always happened. Some authorities have decreased the percentage of their pupils educated in special schools, in line with the recommendations of the 1981 Act; others have found that their special schools are more heavily subscribed than ever. However, across the country as a whole there does seem to be an increase in the number of section 5 assessments undertaken. We will consider some of the reasons for this in the next section.

More recently, statements are no longer necessarily viewed as a universally 'good thing'. Parents have sometimes found that their rights are more restricted, once their youngster has a statement, because there are a limited number of suitable placements for their child within the authority and only a limited amount of cash to provide extra support. The 1980 Education Act, in theory, gave parents more choice over the type of school they could opt for, as open enrolment was encouraged. With a statement, they might find their choice severely circumscribed.

In addition, a statement can sometimes 'label' a child as effectively as some of the older, more emotive terms; being 'statemented' brings with it the problems we described in Chapter 2. Thus the statutory assessment process that results in a statement being issued may not always serve the interests of the child. Another dimension has been provided since the passing of the 1988 Education Reform Act, which has dramatically affected the lives of all schoolchildren and has had differential effects for those children with special needs and those with statements. We shall discuss this in the following section.

Section 5 Assessment: a simplified summary

The LEA signals its intention to undertake a section 5 assessment on the basis of the information it has received. It does this by writing to the parents, asking for their views and giving them 29 days to respond.

After this period, the LEA will then begin the multi-disciplinary assessment by asking for advice from professionals (educational, medical and psychological).

Having received the advice, the LEA will decide whether or not to issue a statement. If it feels that the child does have needs which warrant some form of special provision to be made, it will send the proposed statement to the parents.

Once parents and LEA are happy with the provision on offer, a final statement is issued.

The Education Reform Act 1988

The 1988 Act introduced many wide-ranging changes into the educational system, two of especial significance for children with special needs being the introduction of the National Curriculum and local management of schools (LMS).

The National Curriculum

The introduction of the National Curriculum with its Attainment Targets for each curriculum area and its range of levels within each subject has raised some interesting questions for teachers concerned with children with special needs (see pp. 40–2). The concept of *entitlement* and *access* to the National Curriculum has made teachers look at what they teach to children with special needs, how they teach it and what levels of achievement they should expect from the children.

In special schools, where a detailed structured curriculum was already in place, it has sometimes been necessary to review this to ensure that all areas of the National Curriculum are covered. The teaching requirements for the science curriculum, for example, have meant that some special schools have attempted to introduce more science. Because they have often been pleasantly surprised by the results the National Curriculum with its broader range has come to be seen as a positive step in terms of the *normalization* of the children in their care.

However, for many children with special needs in mainstream settings, whether they hold a statement or not, the advent of the National Curriculum has been problematic and has left teachers with less flexibility. It has prompted concern among many teachers about the large band of children with some degree of learning difficulty who, until recently, were happily studying alongside their peers, but at much lower attainment levels. They are questioning whether the Standard Assessment Tasks (SATs) to be administered to children at 7 and 11 years of age, and the ongoing teacher assessment which accompanies these, can be of benefit for all children or whether some should have been statemented or exempted in some way from the tests.

The guidance from the DES and from the National Curriculum Council (NCC, 1989a, b) suggests that the number of statements should not rise as a result of the introduction of the National Curriculum, nor should children be statemented in order for them to be exempted from testing. For children who are statemented, there are grounds for parts of the National Curriculum to be *modified* or *disapplied*, where it is judged not to be in the child's best interests either to be taught or tested on certain sections or in certain subjects. An example of this might be to modify the 'speaking and listening' component of the English curriculum for a child with hearing difficulties.

Modifications and disapplications of the National Curriculum

For children who hold a statement of their special educational needs, it is possible for the National Curriculum requirements to be modified in a number of ways. This may or may not be written into their statement. Modifications may be made to the *range of subjects* they study (e.g. reduce

---

the number of subjects), the *levels* (e.g. a change in the level of Attainment Targets the child works towards), the *time* spent (e.g. change or specify the time spent on each subject), by *adding or replacing* subjects (e.g. replacing National Curriculum subjects with non-National Curriculum subjects) and finally the *assessment arrangements*. This final change may mean a total or partial disapplication of the requirement for the child to be assessed on the SATs (Standard Assessment Tasks).

For a non-statemented child, it is possible for headteachers to apply for a disapplication of the requirement to test a child under SATs. However, the DES made it clear that this should be a rare occurrence and there should be good reasons for a child to be excluded from the tests. If the child might be able to show some appropriate performance in relation to the statements of attainment being assessed, then he should be allowed to participate. The government circulars allow for full or partial disapplication of the SATs requirements.

There is also the facility for a *temporary exception* to be made for an individual child not to be subject to National Curriculum requirements. These are not encouraged, and require the head of the school to submit to the LEA the reasons why the child is to be exempted, for how long this is intended and the arrangements that will be made to reintroduce the child to the National Curriculum after the exemption period. An example of a genuine case might be a child who is newly arrived to the country, with very little English, whose chronological age puts him in Year 2. There would be little to be gained and potential damage done if the child was presented with SATs alongside the other children.

Temporary exceptions from the National Curriculum

Headteachers may feel that in certain cases it is justified to apply for a *temporary exception* for a child from the assessment, recording and reporting required under the National Curriculum. The DFE advises that this should happen only in exceptional circumstances. The temporary exceptions come under two categories: a *general direction* and a *special direction*. (A 'direction' is the term used in the regulations to refer to a formal written document stating that a pupil requires temporary exception from any or all of the provisions of the National Curriculum as they apply to that pupil.)

A *general direction* is one where the headteacher believes that the pupil will be able to follow the full National Curriculum within six months of the date of the direction. Examples might include children newly arrived from a different educational system, children who have been in hospital, children who have been educated at home or excluded from school and need time to adjust, or those who have temporary but severe emotional problems and need special arrangements.

A *special direction* applies only when the head believes the pupil requires assessment under the 1981 Education Act and is at the early stages of this process.

These are some of the specific problems which may face primary teachers in attempting to reconcile National Curriculum requirements with the teaching of children with special needs. A more pervasive and fundamental problem is that of how teachers use their time in the classroom and how they establish their priorities. The requirement to cover all areas of the National Curriculum and to ensure that children are exposed to the necessary learning experiences has meant that certain areas of practice have had to be discontinued or substantially reduced. For instance, there may be less time spent on thematic project work or on hearing children read. Moreover, classes often lose the support of floating teachers or special needs teachers because these teachers now have to take out groups for practical science tasks, or to administer the SATs. In such situations special needs teaching and support for individual pupils has to be withdrawn. Teachers are likely to feel that they have no spare capacity to meet the needs of these children. Therefore, by and large, the requirements of the National Curriculum have often resulted in less special needs help being available in mainstream schools. This is the sad but inevitable consequence of special needs children being seen as low priority.

Local management of schools (LMS)

The second major change brought about by the 1988 Education Reform Act is the delegation of budgets from local authorities to schools. Heads are in some cases managing very large budgets and have been given more power to decide how to spend this money.

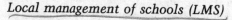

145

> ### *Formula funding*
>
> The amount of money that schools are entitled to is decided mainly by the number and age of pupils on roll, along with a variety of other factors, such as special needs and deprivation weightings. All these factors are considered and the LEA then reaches a formula which it applies to all schools and so decides the amount of money each school is entitled to. All LEA proposals for formula funding must follow certain guidelines laid down by the DES (now the DFE) and have to be submitted to the DFE for approval.

Along with this management change, the Education Reform Act has positively encouraged schools to become more competitive, to ensure that they provide what parents are believed to want. New categories of school have been introduced, such as city technology colleges (CTCs) and grant-maintained schools (GMS). These have served to make state schools become more conscious of the need to market themselves. Recent government initiatives have made it abundantly clear that the government wants to see schools diversify, in order to satisfy parental choice, and the main avenue for them to achieve this is to opt out of local authority control and become grant-maintained. In such a situation, pupils with special needs and disruptive pupils are not always seen as good selling points.

At present there is no extra weighting, in terms of the amount of money per pupil, given to pupils with special needs. Schools are expected to provide for pupils with special needs from within the overall funds allocated to them. Some local authorities have been able to build special needs factors into the formulae they use to distribute budgets but these amounts rarely enable schools to provide adequate support. Special needs pupils and disruptive pupils both take a great deal of teacher time and, in a school environment which is becoming cost–benefit orientated, they may well come to be viewed as non-desirable or even economically non-viable.

Allied to this problem is the requirement, also introduced in the 1988 Act, for schools to publish their results. This is intended to increase their accountability and to give parents data on which to base their choice of school. Results include the SATs results, attendance figures and, in the case of secondary schools, GCSE and A-level examination results. Once again, special needs pupils will not be very attractive to schools who are struggling to improve their overall profile in the community! Until real recognition, at a national level, is given to the importance of teaching special needs pupils and acknowledgement that relative, rather than absolute, achievements are valid measures, then the situation will, we fear, worsen.

To summarize, the Education Reform Act 1988 has put increased pressures on schools trying to meet the needs of children with difficulties. The National Curriculum, although securing a broader curriculum for many children, has meant that teacher time has been diverted to other required activities. Local management of schools (LMS) gives schools, in theory, the autonomy and flexibility to choose how to spend their money. However, in practice, it is likely to result in a poorer deal for children with special needs.

The Children Act 1989

The Children Act is a major piece of legislation that superseded much of the existing child care legislation and has sought to change the emphasis of preceding legislation by making the child's needs paramount. It has implications for parents, health authorities, voluntary bodies and Education Departments as well as fundamentally affecting Social Services Departments and the legal system. In this book we can only highlight key areas affected by the Act and speculate a little as to the outcome for children with special needs.

Key areas of the Act

Any decisions about the child in terms of care, home circumstances, legal status, education or health must consider the child's needs first and foremost. This may seem obvious, but in fact previous legislation and existing ethos and practice gave far more emphasis to the rights of parents and local authorities. Wherever possible, bearing in mind the child's age, intellectual ability or developmental levels, the child's wishes must be taken into consideration. For us as workers in the field of education this means that we must ensure that the child's views are obtained, wherever possible, that other ways of assessing the child's feelings are considered (for example, looking at his behaviour patterns in certain settings) and that the child's expressed views are considered alongside other evidence.

The child's wishes in terms of his preference for schools may be an important part of an assessment under the Education Act 1981. An adolescent who is being proposed as a candidate for a residential special school may well have strong views on what should happen to him, and so careful negotiations will be needed to ensure that a sensible decision is made about his future.

New regulations governing child protection procedures and policies again shift the emphasis away from the rights of parents and of local authorities. The Act tries to give a balanced view, reflecting, on the one hand, the outcomes of individual cases of abuse, where children have suffered severe abuse and even death at the hands of their parents or carers. However, on the other hand, the powers of local authorities have also been altered following the Butler-Sloss Inquiry (1988) into the Cleveland child abuse cases, where doctors and social workers were judged to have acted too hastily in taking children away from their parents when abuse was suspected. For all professionals who work with children, it is vitally important that they know, understand and follow the correct procedures with any suspected cases of child abuse.

New court orders affecting children are introduced in the Act. Many of these are too complex to detail here but they affect familiar orders such as 'custody' and 'access', which have been renamed as 'residence' and 'contact' orders.

Parental responsibility receives a great deal of attention in the Act, as again there has been a *shift away from the rights that parents have over their children, in favour of the responsibilities which rest on them.* There are also changes in the law governing which people can have 'parental responsibility'. This is a new, legally defined term. Only the child's natural mother has parental responsibility for the child if the parents are not legally married at the time of the child's birth. The child's father can, however, acquire parental responsibility by signing a legal agreement or by going to court. Other people can also acquire parental responsibility for a child and so there can, in some cases, be several people who are looking after the child's interests. Examples might be grandparents who have had a child living with them for several years, or foster parents who play a large part in the child's life and with whom the child lives. For children who are in the care of the local authority (or who are being 'accommodated' by the local authority, as the law now phrases it), parental responsibility can be held jointly by the parents and the authority.

The subject of parental rights is one with which schools and teachers should be familiar. At a time when parents' rights regarding education are seen as crucial and their involvement in their child's education is positively encouraged, it is important for schools to be clear about who has responsibility for each child. In this way they can ensure that contact is made with the relevant people in terms of general school activities, such as parents' evenings, governors' meetings and the sharing of written reports on the children. It will also be relevant to decision-making affecting individual children, e.g. starting a section 5 assessment or excluding a child.

Finally, the Children Act attempts to identify *children in need* and *places duties on local authorities in terms of these children.* The definition is a broad one, encompassing factors such as deprivation, split families, children from ethnic minorities as well as special needs in the educational sense of the term. The Act obliges all agencies to work together to ensure that these children are identified and resources are 'activated' to meet their needs. It is early to judge how this will affect the lives of children with special educational needs but suffice it to say that this is another piece of legislation enacted without additional resources to enable it. In sum, the Children Act 1989 has radically affected the law in the United Kingdom and the way it deals with children. It has also changed the emphasis in terms of the shared responsibilities that parents and carers and local authorities have for children. It also affirms that when any changes in a child's circumstances are necessitated, then the needs of the child shall be of paramount importance.

LOCAL EDUCATION AUTHORITIES

Special needs departments within LEAs

The role that local education authorities play regarding the administration and management of schools is likely to change radically during the 1990s. As many schools decide to opt out of local authority control and apply for grant-maintained status and as others take more and more responsibility for their budgets, staffing and day-to-day running via LMS, local authorities will need to determine what part they have to play. This is particularly pertinent in the area of special needs because it may become one of the few remaining areas of responsibility which falls to the LEA. On a pragmatic level, particularly in the light of current legislation, it will be necessary for many authorities to define special needs policy and spending even more precisely than has hitherto been the case. While they still have responsibility for children with special needs, local authorities will need to re-examine their patterns of provision for these pupils. The funding of special schools is under review and they will soon have their own locally managed budgets, under LMS, in line with mainstream schools, called LMSS. Special needs is one of the areas in which LEAs retain responsibility but in practice this might merely mean fulfilling statutory duties under the Education Act 1981 and monitoring the special provision purchased, in effect, from schools.

Patterns of provision

At the present time, local authorities provide for special needs children in various ways. Policy decisions are influenced by the size, geography and population distribution of the authority. In large rural counties, specialized provision of a particular type may be a great distance away from the homes of some children. If distances are too great for a comfortable taxi drive each morning and afternoon, then until recently residential provision has been recommended. Nowadays, both local authorities and parents are more likely to seek to provide specialized resources within local schools, wherever this is possible.

Conversely, in large conurbations, where there may be a strong history of special school provision, it requires a positive policy decision to divert existing resources away from established and relatively local special schools into neighbourhood mainstream schools. This can be achieved in a number of ways, and different authorities have experimented with various methods to discover which will best meet children's needs.

Examples of authorities that have made *positive* policy decisions and have experimented with their special provision include Banbury, Oxfordshire, which has grouped schools into 'sectors' (Jones, 1983; Sayer, 1983, 1985). One or more secondary schools joined with their feeder primary schools to form a unit to which special resources are allocated. Decisions about the distribution and use of these resources are made jointly by headteachers, support staff and administrators. Dessent (1988) feels that this model has a great deal to commend it but also that it is 'unlikely to gain much momentum if it is restricted to meeting special needs alone' (p. 36).

Nowadays, with the greater responsibility they have for their own budgets, schools can co-operate and share services. In this way other traditional LEA services, such as caretaking and cleaning, in-service provision and staffing agencies have been delegated. In such a situation Dessent's warning is more likely to be heeded. It may become much easier for schools to set up joint planning groups to administer the shared resources allocated to them.

A very similar model was proposed in the Fish Report (1985), which considered special educational provision and support within the Inner London Education Authority (since abolished). This report introduced the notion of the 'clustering' of groups of schools, within geographical areas, along with specialist support and provision. However, the report warned that any such change in provision should ensure that 'the principal aim of changes should be to delegate responsibilities within firm guidelines established by the authority to the nearest practical point of service delivery'.

Things have changed since 1985 and now local authorities are in no position to issue 'firm guidelines' to headteachers or to clusters of schools on any subject, as power shifts towards headteachers and governing bodies. The current structural changes may result in there being no cohesive special needs policy or quality assurance within authorities and no means of ensuring that such policies are effectively implemented. For LEAs and schools to continue to work together effectively, it is vital that all parties see the value of clear, consistent, agreed policies and high levels of quality assurance in regard to provision for children with special needs.

Over the past ten years, since the 1981 Act has been in operation, the means of accessing extra support services within local authorities has varied, with policy being decided at a local level. In some authorities, for a child to receive any service (within education) that is different from that which the majority of his peers are receiving, he will need to have been issued with a statement and therefore to have had a formal assessment. In other authorities, there are some services which can be made available to children without the need of a statement. Over the next ten years, however, as LEAs have a much reduced budget at their disposal, they may use 'statements' as a very tight, formal and indeed legal method of deciding which children should benefit from the residual resources. In such a scenario, support services, such as specialist visiting teachers, will become tightly linked to named children with statements. The corollary of this is that the more general support and advice often provided by these services may have to be curtailed. For some schools and teachers, this may mean that they have to look to support within their own schools, between schools, or 'buy in' advice and help from outside sources. Such procedures may in the future be more tightly controlled by legislation and not be left to local policy decision-making bodies.

Policy-making within schools

With decisions about special needs teaching being progressively left to groups of schools or to individual schools, let us consider some of the key issues which must be addressed by headteachers and their members of staff.

Staffing

Decisions about responsibilities within schools and the remuneration attached to them are now made jointly by heads and governing bodies. National Curriculum requirements have forced heads in some schools to consider appointing co-ordinators for each of the core curriculum areas, and in others for each of the Key Stages. Some schools may have opted for both. The size of school is a crucial factor, particularly in the primary phase, where small numbers mean limited funding and less flexibility. For many primary schools, LMS has meant not being able to afford a special needs co-ordinator with non-teaching time built into her job description. The popular alternative is to ask teachers to act as co-ordinators while also being a full-time class teacher.

The practice of a special needs co-ordinator will be governed by existing policies and the arrangements that result from them. Where withdrawal arrangements exist, the special needs teacher will probably undertake the bulk of the support teaching. If in-class support is preferred, then the special needs teacher may share her time between classes, supporting individuals within the class. Some schools prefer to target their limited resources on particular years or groups of children. Perhaps the Year 1 children may be selected to have learning support as the classroom assistant support available in most reception classes disappears.

In some schools, where no special needs help exists at all, the well-worn cliché that 'all teachers are teachers of special needs' applies. Whether they are able to carry out this role effectively depends on the availability of training, resources and support.

Difficulties can occur within schools if provision is not planned in a co-ordinated, whole-school approach. It is important that the intended function of extra help is understood and accepted by all those working in the school. The Fish Report noted that 'Problems arise because many schools either plan provision on the curing assumption or on the segregation assumption.' Both militate against good practice.

The 'curing assumption' is that a learning difficulty resides entirely within the child and special teaching is required in order to treat him effectively. Once he is 'cured', then he can rejoin his classmates. (This view is obviously not consistent with our assertion that good special needs teaching is no different from good general teaching.) Teachers holding the curing assumption are likely to be disappointed when children rejoin their classes and still require extra help.

The 'segregation assumption', which seeks to segregate children with difficulties, also gives credence to the notion that the problems lie mainly within the child. Segregation, it is thought, is logical on the grounds that special needs children are 'different', and it is organizationally expedient to separate them from the other children in the school. The existence of these guiding assumptions behind policy decisions on special needs provision shows clearly how the fundamental belief systems that operate within the school influence practice. We shall consider this further in the next section.

Policy development

Schools are required to produce policy statements covering many areas of school life: for example, equal opportunities, the teaching of reading, parental involvement and discipline. In order to ensure that a policy document is workable and useful to all concerned, certain key stages in the development of that policy should be observed. This applies equally to special needs policies. As we have seen, the fundamental beliefs behind any special needs policy statement will crucially affect the way resources are deployed within a school and the priority that is given to children with special needs. Increasingly, schools will be deciding their own ways forward, via their school development plans (SDPs), and all teachers, including those who are newly qualified, will be expected to contribute to these plans. In view, of this, the following section may be helpful.

A model for policy development

To help individual teachers conceptualize the process of policy development, we would like to introduce a model which has been used effectively in schools in the areas of special needs and behaviour management (Facherty *et al.*, 1992; Luton *et al.*, 1991). It is known as the 'Three P's model' of policy formation because it involves writing down the *philosophy, principles and practice* to which everyone will work. The first stage is to agree on a statement of the *philosophical beliefs* that are shared by those who will operate the policy (e.g. 'Parents play a vital role in the life of any school'; 'Schools should encourage respect for others and for oneself'). Achieving consensus on this can prove a useful staff development exercise in its own right! Once these philosophical beliefs have been stated, the group can move on to the next phase, which is to agree upon a set of *principles* deriving from the philosophy. These should be general guides to practice. The generality is necessary because it is almost impossible to define procedures for all aspects of school life; staff need to be able to interpret policy by reference to guidelines or principles. An example of a principle might be: 'Parents should be involved, at the earliest possible point, in matters to do with individual learning problems.'

The final stage of policy definition relates to day-to-day *practice* and specifies procedures by which a common approach and smooth running within the school can be ensured. It covers both routine events, such as dinner-time routines and manners, and also more critical events, such as when and how to begin the formal statementing process. An example of practice might therefore be: 'When a child earns 20 merit points, a certificate is sent home to parents.'

By constructing a policy document in which each stage clearly and logically follows on from the preceding stage, any extension or alteration is easily made. This ought to be a regular occurrence for any document that really relates to practice in a school, because government or LEA directives necessitate fairly frequent changes in policy. For example, a school's policy on assessment may need to be altered as more or different regulations governing National Curriculum assessment are issued. When deciding on the format of policy documents this need for regular review and updating should be borne in mind.

Priorities in primary schools have been changing so quickly that teachers can understandably wonder what is likely to be the next 'flavour of the month'. In such an uncertain climate, in which special needs policy may well be assigned a low priority or may be subject to the changing whims of the headteacher, individual class teachers more than ever need to be clear about their own beliefs and aspirations for children with special needs, and about the policies they wish to pursue in their classes. Therefore, when policy is not clear within a school, or when an individual teacher is left to her own devices, the Three P's model can help to clarify thinking.

CHAPTER SUMMARY

For many teachers, policy decisions within education come from such a plethora of sources that they find it impossible to make sense of it all. This is certainly true for newly qualified teachers and particularly pertinent in the area of special needs. Recent government legislation has radically affected the lives of special needs children both directly and indirectly. This chapter attempts to provide a guide to what can seem a morass of legislation, policy decisions and directives. We outlined the major legislation, such as the 1981 Education Act, which specifically addresses questions relating to special needs children. We also considered more general legislation, such as the Education Reform Act 1988 and the Children Act 1989, and looked at the specific effects on children with special needs.

We then considered the diminishing roles of LEAs. It begins to seem as if LEAs will retain responsibility for very little. One of their remaining responsibilities thus far is the education of children with special needs. We considered the traditional LEA role in determining patterns of provision and have speculated about how this may change in the future. In the next section, we addressed the issue of policy development within schools. Now that schools are more self-governing, the process of deciding priorities, including the priority that is assigned to special needs, will be crucial. We looked at the implications that policy decisions on special needs may have for staffing and roles within schools and, in turn, what effect these might have on individual class teachers. In case class teachers are left in something of a policy vacuum regarding special needs, we provided a model of policy definition, which may help them to clarify their own views and to see a way forward, should nothing more coherent be forthcoming from within the school.

SUGGESTIONS FOR FURTHER READING

Audit Commission/HMI (1992) *Getting In on the Act. Provision for Pupils with Special Educational Needs: The National Picture.* London: HMSO. A clear, comprehensive survey of special needs practice across the country in the early 1990s. It is likely to be influential in future government thinking.

Dessent, T. (1987) *Making the Ordinary School Special.* Basingstoke: Falmer. A radical book, at the time of writing, it provides a useful perspective on the relationships between special and mainstream education.

Goacher, B., Evans, J., Welton, J. and Wedell, K. (1988) *Policy and Provision for Special Educational Needs: Implementing the 1981 Education Act.* London: Cassell. Based on detailed research undertaken in the early 1980s, this book provides comprehensive analysis of these areas of study and makes some proposals for improvement.

Solity, J. E. and Raybould, E. (1988) *A Teacher's Guide to Special Needs: A Positive Response to the 1981 Education Act.* Milton Keynes: Open University Press. A detailed text which provides useful information on teaching and assessment and on preparing reports. The book also provides useful advice on working with parents.

Thomas, G. and Feiler, A. (1988) *Planning for Special Needs: A Whole-School Approach.* Oxford: Basil Blackwell. This book provides an overview of the changes that have taken place over the past decade in special needs education. It suggests different ways of looking at children with special needs in terms of whole-school and classroom approaches.

White, R., Carr, P. and Lowe, N. (1990) *A Guide to the Children Act 1989.* London: Butterworth. An introductory text which deals with each of the central thrusts of the Children Act in a readable, comprehensible manner.

CHAPTER 10

Looking into the future: secondary transfer and the future for special needs pupils

CHAPTER OVERVIEW

A crucial stage in a pupil's life is the point of secondary transfer; this is all the more important for special needs children. In this chapter, we will examine how teachers can assist parents in choosing an appropriate school and in ensuring that what has been learnt about the child is passed on to the secondary school in a form which is relevant and useful. We will also examine how the pupil can be assisted in preparing for the change of school.

In the latter part of the chapter, we will offer some speculative observations on the development of special needs as we approach the end of the millennium. We adopt a positive outlook, while recognizing the realities with which education is faced. Most importantly, we will stress the importance of the contributions that can be made by individual schools and teachers.

SECONDARY TRANSFER

We all have vivid memories of our first weeks in secondary school as we tried to come to terms with the sheer size of the place, the number of teachers and pupils, the complexities of the timetable and the frightening strangeness of it all. Most people seem to remember this period as one of excitement mixed with apprehension and uncertainty. The new pupils have just left the relative security of their primary school in which they had become big fish in a small pond to find themselves minnows in a big sea. These emotions and reactions can become all the more intense for the special needs child, who has additional worries and concerns.

The whole approach to easing pupils into their new schools has improved considerably as secondary schools have been forced into marketing themselves and into competing for children. Links with the feeder primaries have been developed allowing pupils to visit their new schools, to meet their teachers, to identify where they will be based, to find out where the toilets are, to be told what they should do on their first day and to gain a general flavour of what awaits them. Preparation will also be carried out by the primary teachers; this is of crucial importance for the special needs child.

The early steps

In most authorities, parents begin the process of selecting a school at least a year before transfer. Statemented pupils usually have first choice for particular secondary schools, assuming it has been decided that their needs can be met in such establishments. For pupils who have special needs, but who do not have a statement, this advantage generally does not exist, and it would therefore be strongly advisable to start the process of choosing an appropriate school early in the penultimate year of primary schooling.

Reviewing the statemented child's needs

The headteacher is responsible for conducting an *annual review* of each statemented child. In general terms, this is a meeting during which the school lets the parents know how it has attempted to meet the child's needs as determined through the original statutory assessment and listed on the current statement. When the time comes for transfer to secondary school, this review meeting should take place well before the school selection deadline. Parents will then have the relevant information to hand and plenty of time to visit schools and to seek further advice, if necessary. In reporting back to the parents, in addition to providing a report from the child's teachers, the school may also draw upon the advice of other colleagues who have acted in a supporting role, such as specialist advisory staff. This may mean health authority personnel and, in the case of a child transferring to secondary school, usually his educational psychologist. A central part of the review should involve asking the parents to comment on how *they* have viewed the child's progress.

The purpose of the review is to establish whether the child's needs are being met by the existing arrangements or whether there is a requirement to implement changes, which may involve altering the statement. This is clearly an important matter as the child approaches secondary transfer. The psychologist can offer an independent view and advise the parents on the types of provision that will meet their child's needs, and what kind of provision is available in the authority. It is not the psychologist's responsibility to allocate resources, but to offer clear advice on how the child's needs can be met, on the basis of the evidence supplied and her own assessment of the child.

In ideal circumstances, the parents should have a range of choices which might include:

- a straightforward placement in a secondary school;
- a placement in a secondary school supported by an integration assistant;
- a placement in a unit or facility attached to a mainstream school;
- a transfer to a special school.

In reality, this range of choice is rarely available or appropriate. Secondary transfer is certainly the point at which the gap between the ideal and the real availability of resources comes into sharp focus. The review should give the parents a clear and honest picture of what is required for their child and what is available for them to visit.

Once the parents have visited or considered the options open to them and selected a school on the basis of advice from the professionals involved, the LEA may then amend the child's statement accordingly. This is sometimes done by means of the annual review document. Where the chosen school is particularly popular, the child with a statement has a distinct advantage and should secure a place. Increasingly, however, it will be the case that such children will be accepted only if the resourcing necessary to meet their needs is written into the statement and provided by the LEA.

Writing a report for a review

The teacher's role in the review is to provide the parents and the LEA with a detailed report, particularly regarding those aspects relating to the child's special educational needs. This is usually presented in writing, with the teacher elaborating on it orally and providing any further information that may be requested at the review. In effect, this will be a summary and overview of the data collected on the child, hence the value of keeping simple but consistent and readily accessible records which chart the child's progress in response to changes in the style of teaching or the use of particular materials. The task of compiling a report for an annual review will be made all the easier if the teacher has taken time to step back and to examine the growing data, at least on a half-termly basis. It is often useful to share the data and the ongoing conclusions with another colleague or a specialist support teacher.

When compiling the report for the annual review the teacher should not feel that the expectations are the same as when completing a statutory 'Educational Advice' as part of an initial assessment under section 5 of the 1981 Education Act. Instead, the teacher will be reporting on how the child has progressed over the year and, equally important, what has been learnt by the teachers on how best to meet the child's needs. Solity and Raybould (1988, pp. 110–20), discussing what should be included in an Educational Advice, have provided a useful checklist. Despite the differences between this and an annual review, we would recommend this checklist as valuable for the teacher writing a report for a review. The following guidelines are drawn from it.

- Is the information based on facts and data with which you are *honestly satisfied*?
- Is it likely that other colleagues would come to similar conclusions with the same data?
- Does the report cover all *relevant* areas, i.e. those that are specified in the statement related to the child's needs?
- Are factual matters separated from *interpretation and opinion*? The latter aspects are important but should be included separately from factual data.
- Is there a *balance* in the report between the positives and the negatives and between the successes and failures?
- Does the child still *come through* in the report? There is always the difficulty, in writing such reports, that the text becomes over-clinical and the parents have difficulty in recognizing their own child.
- Will the parents be able to *read and understand* the report? If they have difficulties with reading then this needs to be taken into account. Equally, if the parents speak and read a language other than English, the report should (resources allowing) be translated into the appropriate language.
- Finally, as a parent *would you be happy to receive this report on your child*?

In talking through the report, the emphasis should be on describing what has gone on over the last year. Almost inevitably, however, the teacher will be asked by the parents for a view on the appropriate school for the child. This is a recognition of the fact that she will know the child extremely well; the problem is that she will have a limited knowledge of the available secondary provision. In such circumstances, it is most helpful for teachers to concentrate on what the child needs and to be honest about their level of knowledge concerning the available range of schools.

The headteacher's responsibility will be to chair the review and to provide an overview for the parents of how the child has progressed over the years. The headteacher will also be responsible for advising the LEA, through the completion of a standard form, on any recommendations or amendments that should be made to the existing statement. The duty to carry out the review in an appropriate fashion and at a suitable time is one which headteachers must take seriously for statemented children.

Reviewing the needs of the non-statemented child

There are legal obligations which determine the process of review for pupils with statements. The fate of special needs children who do not have a statement depends on the individual school's policies and arrangements for special needs children. The circumstances of secondary transfer dictate the same requirements: to ensure that the parents are briefed well before the deadline for secondary choice selection. The requirements for schools to report to *all* parents are now more stringent, and this has served to reinforce good practice in regard to special needs pupils.

The end of year 5, when teachers offer parents the chance to discuss their child's progress, is the ideal opportunity to review the special needs child's progress in detail. Here again, the benefits of detailed record-keeping will come to the fore. The teacher's task will be to give the parents an overview and to suggest what this means in terms of the child's needs at secondary level. In formulating this view the teacher will obviously need to seek the guidance of senior staff and particularly the special needs support teacher. If it is possible, the teacher will find it useful to discuss the case at an advisory level with the school's attached psychologist or support teacher.

The teacher will rarely be expected to provide a detailed written report as in the case of a formal review of a child with a statement. It is nonetheless necessary for the teacher to go through the same process to ensure that the parents have a clear picture of their child's needs and requirements at secondary level. In effect, the teacher is advising parents on what should be on their shopping list when looking around prospective secondary schools. Many parents will have clear views about the type of school they want for their children as a result of their religious or cultural beliefs; in fact, these may be their overriding consideration. This must be taken into account when offering advice to parents about the range of aspects which need to be considered. At a practical level, it will be necessary to allocate a longer time for meeting the parents and to offer them further meetings should they want to discuss their feelings after visiting prospective schools.

PREPARING THE CHILD FOR SECONDARY TRANSFER

Year 6 teachers have the task of preparing their pupils for the transfer to secondary school. In general, most teachers do this by working alongside the staff from the secondaries and by talking through issues with their pupils. It is important to listen to children's worries and anxieties, as well as sharing in their excitement, before offering information, reassurance and encouragement. The special needs child will probably need greater levels of support on a personal basis. We offer the following as suggestions to be considered when planning a programme of support for the child:

- Work alongside the parents and ensure that the same messages are being communicated. For this it is necessary to *establish a communication system* so that all information, particularly about matters worrying the child, is shared.
- Arrange to *visit the secondary school* and to meet the receiving staff, particularly if it is an unfamiliar school. This will be a chance to find out about the school, so that the child's questions can be answered and also to check for yourself that the school will be able to meet the child's needs. It would also be helpful, if possible, to establish what information receiving staff would find valuable in planning their programmes for the child.
- *Visit the school with the child* and use this as an opportunity to find answers to the child's questions. It is helpful to prepare for the visit by talking with the child about what he already knows of the school and establishing his personal checklist.
- Complete some follow-up work on the new school and *encourage the child to talk* to the class or group about the school.
- Identify which *children will be moving to the same school* and set group work and tasks related to the transfer.
- *Involve the child in producing a report on himself* which details not only his difficulties but also his achievements. This draws heavily on the Record of Achievement approach and the concept of involving the pupil in determining suitable programmes of work and management. It may also be reassuring for the child to accept that the new school will *know all about him*.
- Produce a *hand-over report* on the child to be passed on to the receiving school and share this with the parents and child, where appropriate (suggestions for this are on pp. 162–3).
- Arrange to *visit the school during the first term*. This acts as

a link between phases and also an opportunity for the teacher
to be reassured (hopefully) that her work is being built upon.

There may be other things teachers could do; our list is not
exhaustive. On the other hand, not all the recommended steps may
be possible or advisable, according to individual circumstances. It also
has to be recognized that certain children may wish to cope with the
transfer on their own or merely with the support of their parents.
The essential task for teachers, though, whatever else they do to help
the transfer, is to pass adequate records on to the receiving school.

TRANSFERRING INFORMATION TO THE NEW SCHOOL

There will be differences between statemented and non-statemented
pupils in terms of the information which the school will pass on.

In the case of statemented pupils, the statement, in a sense, moves
with the child. The LEA will be responsible for deciding whether any
amendments are necessary in the light of the last annual review and
the transfer to a secondary school. Additionally, responsibility rests
with the LEA for ensuring that the new school is aware of the statement, although this is usually completed on a school to school basis.
The transfer of information should include the teacher's report and/or
the annual review document.

In the case of a non-statemented child with special needs, there is
a danger that what has been achieved at the primary level will not be
passed on to the secondary school. We would argue, therefore, that to
ensure that the work of primary staff is built upon, a package of information needs to be transferred in the case of *all* special needs pupils.
The emphasis should be on ensuring that the details of the child's
special educational needs and what has been learnt about meeting
those needs is made available. This will not only prevent the wastage
involved in 'starting afresh', it will reassure parents.

Preparing a hand-over report

Year 6 teachers, in consultation with the headteacher, might
consider the following questions when compiling a hand-
over report:

- Does the child have a *statement of special educational needs*?

If yes, send a copy of the statement and attach copies of the

---

most recent annual review and any teacher reports submitted at the time. Any other relevant reports including, for example, medical reports should also be appended.

- What is the *nature* of the pupil's special educational needs?
- What *difficulties* does the pupil experience or present?
- Looking back through the pupil's records, *for how long* have these difficulties been recognized?
- In *what ways do these difficulties impact* on:
  - the pupil;
  - the peer group;
  - teaching and non-teaching staff;
  - the child's parents.

- How have teachers managed to *meet these needs*? Give examples of particular programmes, be they learning, behavioural or social, etc.
- Have any *physical modifications* or adaptations been necessary?
- Describe the child's achievements in terms of the *National Curriculum*. Were any modifications or adaptations necessary?
- Are any *other professionals* actively involved with the child? If so, list their names, contact addresses and roles.
- Are there *any other approaches, techniques or materials* which have been found to work with this child?
- Have there been any *glaring failures* with this pupil which the receiving school should know about to prevent an unproductive repetition?
- What is the pupil *good at* and what does he like to do?
- How *realistic* a picture does the child have about his difficulties?
- Arising out of work with the child, are there any general remarks or *pieces of advice* which you would like to pass on to secondary colleagues?
- What roles have the *child's parents* played to date and what are they likely to wish to contribute at secondary level?
- Finally, as a parent, if this was your child moving to a new school, are there any other matters or pieces of information which you would like to pass on?

Teachers' workloads are already far too great. The question of expediency is therefore very relevant when deciding on (a) the amount of time that can be devoted to the completion of such a report and (b) the likelihood of its actually being read. The aim should be to make it brief, readable and easy to use. Our suggestions have been based on what we know to be useful for receiving teachers and what is viable.

Finally, we would re-emphasize the value of primary and secondary colleagues working together, particularly in connection with special needs pupils. Exchanges of information about working practices will be beneficial and will certainly facilitate smooth transitions for pupils. .

THE FUTURE FOR SPECIAL NEEDS CHILDREN

It is ten years since the 1981 Act came into force and the impact of the Warnock Report started to be felt in schools. The strong emphasis initially placed on special needs has since been eroded by the Education Reform Act and a succession of changes that have placed heavy demands on teachers. Thus the impact of LMS, the National Curriculum and major demands of accountability have meant a definite downgrading for special needs.

Prior to this avalanche of legislation, there were considerable variations across LEAs in the interpretation of the 1981 Education Act. Some operated on the basis of statementing relatively large numbers of children, including those transferring to special education and those remaining in mainstream schools. Other authorities chose instead to make resources readily available to mainstream pupils without the cumbersome requirement of pursuing a statutory assessment and issuing a statement. The latter were, in effect, operating a minimal statementing policy, the success of which was dependent upon the levels of available resources. Significant levels of integration were, however, rarely achieved, basically because the 1981 Education Act did not fund special needs separately. The expectation was apparently that this piece of radical and pervasive legislation could be implemented using existing resources.

The future for LEAs

As this book is nearing completion, the death knell for LEAs, as we know them, is being sounded. There is pressure on schools to pursue grant-maintained status and, as a result, to receive direct funding from central rather than local government. Schools remaining within the current LEA structure are being given increased responsibilities for the management of their budgets (LMS) and this option is being extended to special schools (LMSS). One of the few areas of responsibility which seems likely to be retained by LEAs is that of special needs.

It seems unlikely that there will be any government U-turns in special needs policy (a decision to renege on the philosophical and practical commitments of the Education Act 1981 would be politically unacceptable). But it does seem likely, as recommended in the Audit Commission Report (1992), that there will need to be improvements in the procedures adopted by authorities and schools and the efficiency with which the Act is administered, if the intentions of the Act are to be honoured.

The funds must be available to support statements of special educational need, particularly when financial control is withdrawn from LEAs. It seems likely that the requirement of statements for mainstream pupils will increase as a way of ensuring the resources necessary to meet their needs. Any attempts to accelerate integration, for example by establishing a unit for special education in a mainstream school, will succeed only if the school's governing body knows that the facility will be guaranteed proper funding.

In the increasingly tough world of educational finance it is unlikely that the 'goodwill' on which a lot of work with special needs pupils has been based will survive. Undoubtedly most schools recognize that they have responsibilities to special needs pupils, particularly those with learning or behaviour problems, but this commitment will not survive a lack of adequate and protected funding.

Another, and more worrying, threat to successful integration of special needs pupils is the requirement laid on schools to publish their academic results. This could affect their willingness to retain or to integrate pupils with learning difficulties. There is already an increase in the number of pupils being excluded for unacceptable behaviour, exclusion being the only practical policy available to headteachers. Unless future legislation addresses the needs of pupils with learning and/or behaviour problems there is a real danger that schools could turn their backs on such children in an attempt to sustain their competitiveness with other schools.

CHAPTER SUMMARY

The transfer from primary to secondary school can be a time of great concern for pupils with special needs. In this chapter, we have presented a range of suggestions which should ease that process. In so doing, we have also highlighted the importance of ensuring that what has been learnt about a child's needs and how to meet these needs should be passed on to the secondary school in a way which is practicable. We have outlined ideas on how this could be undertaken.

Finally, we have offered some speculative observations on the future for special needs children in these times of significant change in education. Whatever the outcome of future legislation, we remain assured that the skills necessary to meet the needs of such children are very much a part of what is necessary for high-quality teaching for all pupils.

SUGGESTIONS FOR FURTHER READING

Solity, J. E. and Raybould, E. (1988) *A Teacher's Guide to Special Needs: A Positive Response to the 1981 Education Act*. Milton Keynes: Open University Press. A valuable and detailed overview of the 1981 Education Act, including helpful sections on the writing of teachers' reports. In addition, the book offers useful explanations of the processing of the Act for individual pupils and details how teachers can make worthwhile contributions.

References

Ainscow, M. and Tweddle, D. (1979) *Preventing Classroom Failure: An Objectives Approach.* Chichester: Wiley.

Ainscow, M. and Tweddle, D. (1984) *Early Learning Skills Analysis.* Chichester: Wiley.

Ainscow, M. and Tweddle, D. (1988) *Encouraging Classroom Success.* London: David Fulton.

Association of Educational Psychologists (1989) *Integration: Problems and Possibilities for Change.* Durham: AEP.

Audit Commission/HMI (1992) *Getting In on the Act. Provision for Pupils with Special Educational Needs: The National Picture.* London: HMSO.

Baker, D. and Bovair, K. (1989) *Making the Special Schools Ordinary?* Volume 1: *Models for the Developing Special School.* Basingstoke: Falmer.

Brophy, J.E. (1983) Classroom organization and management. *Elementary School Journal,* **83**(4), 264–85.

Bull, S.L. and Solity, J.E. (1987) *Classroom Management: Principles to Practice.* London: Croom Helm.

Butler-Sloss, Hon. Dame E. (1988) *Report of the Inquiry into Child Abuse in Cleveland.* London: HMSO.

Cameron, R. (1982) *Portage in the UK.* Windsor: NFER.

Cheeseman, P.L. and Watts, P.E. (1985) *Positive Behaviour Management: A Manual for Teachers.* Beckenham: Croom Helm.

Croll, P. and Moses, D. (1985) *One in Five: The Assessment and Incidence of Special Educational Needs.* London: Routledge & Kegan Paul.

Cunningham, C.C. and Glenn, S.M. (1989) Parental involvement and early intervention. In D. Lane and B. Stratford, *Current Approaches to Down's Syndrome*. London: Holt, Rinehart & Winston.

Day, A. (1989) Reaching out: the background to outreach. In D. Baker and K. Bovair, *Making the Special Schools Ordinary?* Volume 1. Basingstoke: Falmer.

Department of Education and Science (1944) *Education Act*. London: HMSO.

Department of Education and Science (1955) *Report of the Committee on Maladjusted Behaviour* (Underwood Report). London: HMSO.

Department of Education and Science (1970) *Education (Handicapped Children) Act*. London: HMSO.

Department of Education and Science (1978) *Special Educational Needs* (Warnock Report). London: HMSO.

Department of Education and Science (1980) *Education Act*. London: HMSO.

Department of Education and Science (1981) *Education Act*. London: HMSO.

Department of Education and Science (1986) *Education (No. 2) Act*. London: HMSO.

Department of Education and Science (1988) *Education Reform Act*. London: HMSO.

Department of Education and Science (1989) *Discipline in Schools. Report of the Committee of Inquiry Chaired by Lord Elton*. London: HMSO.

Department of Education and Science/Her Majesty's Inspectorate (1989) *Aspects of Primary Education: The Education of Children Under Five*. London: HMSO.

Department of Education and Science (1991) *Statistics Bulletin*, **9/91** (May).

Department of Health (1970) *The Chronically Sick and Disabled Persons Act*. London: HMSO.

Department of Health (1989) *An Introduction to the Children Act*. London: HMSO.

Department of Health (1990) *NHS and Community Care Act*. London: HMSO.

Dessent, T. (1987) *Making the Ordinary School Special*. Basingstoke: Falmer.

Elliott, M. and Marlin, M. (1986) *The Willow Street Kids: It's Your Right to Be Safe*. London: André Deutsch.

Facherty, A., Howes, J. and Turner, C. (1992) What you need is a policy . . . ! *Educational Psychology in Practice*, 7(4), 237.

Fish, J. (1985) *Special Education: The Way Ahead*. Milton Keynes: Open University Press.

Goacher, B., Evans, J., Welton, J. and Wedell, K. (1988) *Policy and Provision for Special Educational Needs: Implementing the 1981 Act*. London: Cassell.

Goodey, C.F. (1991) *Living in the Real World: Families Speak Out about Down's Syndrome*. London: Twenty-one Press.

Hall, J. (1992) Segregation by another name? *Special Children*, **56**, 20–3.

Hegarty, S., Pocklington, K. and Lucas, D. (1981) *Educating Pupils with Special Needs in the Ordinary School*. Chippenham: NFER.

Hegarty, S. (1982) Integration and the comprehensive school. *Education Review*, **14** (special issue).

Hegarty, S. (1987) *Meeting Special Needs in Ordinary Schools*. London: Cassell. 2nd edition 1993.

Jones, N. (1983) The management of integration: the Oxford experience. In P. Booth and P. Potts (eds), *Integrating Special Education*. Oxford: Basil Blackwell.

Jones, N. (1985) Extending the concept of normality. *Education*, **166**(24), 166.

Kanner, L. (1943) Autistic disturbances of affective contact. *Nervous Child*, **2**, 217–53.

Kounin, J.S. (1970) *Discipline and Group Management in Classrooms*. New York: Krieger.

Lask, J. and Lask, B. (1981) *Child Psychiatry and Social Work*. London: Tavistock.

Laslett, R.B. (1977) *Educating Maladjusted Children*. London: Crosby Lockwood Staples.

Lindsay, G. and Miller, A. (1991) *Psychological Services for Primary Schools*. Harlow: Longman.

Lunzer, E.A. and Gardner, K. (1979) *The Effective Use of Reading*. London: Heinemann Schools Council.

Luton, K., Booth, G., Leadbetter, J., Tee, G. and Wallace, F. (1991) *Positive Strategies for Behaviour Management*. Windsor: NFER-Nelson.

Montgomery, D. (1989) *Managing Behaviour Problems*. Sevenoaks: Hodder & Stoughton.

Montgomery, D. (1990) *Children with Learning Difficulties*. London: Cassell.

National Curriculum Council (1989a) *Circular Number 5: Implementing the National Curriculum – Participation by Pupils with Special Educational Needs*. York: NCC.

National Curriculum Council (1989b) *Two: A Curriculum for All. Special Educational Needs in the National Curriculum*. York: NCC.

National Deaf Children's Society (1987) Annual Report and Accounts. London: NDCS.

Norwich, B. (1990) *Reappraising Special Needs Education*. London: Cassell.

Pearson, L. and Lindsay, G. (1986) *Special Needs in the Primary School*. Windsor: NFER-Nelson.

Peryer, T. (1989) The view from the Education Office. In D. Baker and K. Bovair, *Making the Special Schools Ordinary?* Volume 1. Basingstoke: Falmer.

Rutter, M. (1974) The development of infantile autism. *Psychological Medicine*, **4**, 147–63.

Rutter, M. (1975) *Helping Troubled Children*. London: Penguin Books.

Sayer, J. (1983) A comprehensive school for all. In T. Booth and P. Potts (eds), *Integrating Special Education*. Oxford: Basil Blackwell.

Sayer, J. (1985) *What Future for Secondary Schools?* Lewes: Falmer.

Solity, J. E. and Bull, S. (1987) *Special Needs: Bridging the Curriculum Gap*. Milton Keynes: Open University Press.

Solity, J. E. and Raybould, E. (1988) *A Teacher's Guide to Special Needs: A Positive Response to the 1981 Act*. Milton Keynes: Open University Press.

Spence, S. H. and Shepherd, G. (eds) (1983) *Developments in Social Skills Training*. London: Academic Press.

Sprick, R. (1981) *The Solution Book: A Guide to Classroom Discipline*. Henley-on-Thames: Science Research Associates.

Topping, K. (1983) *Educational Systems for Disruptive Pupils*. London: Croom Helm.

Wade, B. and Moore, M. (1987) *Special Children . . . Special Needs: Provision in Ordinary Classrooms*. London: Robert Royce.

Westmacott, E. V. S. and Cameron, R. J. (1981) *Behaviour Can Change*. London: Macmillan.

Wolfendale, S. (1987) *Primary Schools and Special Needs: Policy, Planning and Provision*. London: Cassell. 2nd edition 1992.

NAME INDEX

Ainscow, M. 30, 38, 40, 42, 85
Association of Educational
    Psychologists 13
Audit Commission 141, 165

Baker, D. 17, 18, 19
Booth, G. (Luton et al.) 83, 87,
    90, 153
Bovair, K. 17, 18, 19
Brophy, J. E. 85
Bull, S. L. 26, 53, 81
Butler-Sloss, Hon. Dame E. 148

Cameron, R. J. 127
Cheeseman, P. L. 64, 80
Croll, P. 32
Cunningham, C. C. 133

Day, A. 17
Dessent, T. 26, 30, 133, 150

Elliott, M. 67
Elton, Lord 61
Evans, J. (Goacher et al.) 6, 8,
    29, 133

Facherty, A. 153

Gardner, K. 52
Goacher, B. 6, 8, 29, 133
Goodey, C. F. 118

Hall, J. 8, 20
Hegarty, S. 8, 17, 18
HMI (Her Majesty's Inspectorate)
    133
Howes, J. (Facherty et al.) 153

Jones, N. 30, 150

Kanner, L. 109
Kounin, J. S. 89

171

SUBJECT INDEX

action plans 77, 79
activity sheets 131
adaptation of materials 48, 53
advice
  educational 139, 159
  medical 139
  psychological 139–40
  see also Education Act 1981
age equivalents 129
annual review 157
  headteacher's
      responsibilities 157
  and reports 158–60
  see also Education Act 1981
applied behavioural analysis
      130
assessment and decision-making
      137
assessment over time 123
assessment procedures
  of behaviour 81
  and section 5 procedures 124,
      139–40, 141
  multi-disciplinary 122, 137
  statutory 137

three-stage model 138
assessment through teaching
      42–8, 50, 132, 137
asthma 103–4
Attainment Targets 41, 142
  see also National Curriculum
attitudes of teachers 31–2, 58
Audit Commission Report 141,
      165
autism 109–11

behaviour and learning links 59
behavioural approaches 130–1
  definition of 64
behavioural objectives 38–9, 44,
      53, 131
  and National Curriculum
      40–1
  in practice 41–2
behavioural problems
  and context 58
  and contracts 90
  and individual children 89–91
brain damage 117

173